altars

Bringing Sacred Shrines
Into Your Everyday Life

altars

Bringing Sacred Shrines Into Your Everyday Life

Denise Linn

Ballantine Wellspring™
The Ballantine Publishing Group • New York

This book is dedicated to my husband, David,
and my daughter, Meadow ...
as always, my best friends.

A Ballantine Wellspring™ Book
Published by The Ballantine Publishing Group

Published in the United States by The Ballantine Publishing Group, a division of Random House, Inc., New York, and distributed in Canada by Random House of Canada Limited, Toronto.
Published in Great Britain in 1999 by Ebury Press, Random House UK Ltd.

www. randomhouse.com/BB/

LIBRARY OF CONGRESS CATALOGING-IN-PUBLICATION DATA
Linn, Denise.
Altars: bringing sacred shrines into your everyday life / Denise Linn.—1st American ed.
p. cm.
ISBN 0-345-43446-3 (alk. paper)
1. Altars. 2. Household shrines. 3. Spiritual life.
I. Title.
BL602.L56 1999
291.3'7—dc21 99–28074

Interior design by Ruth Prentice
Special photography by Patricia Ridenour
Picture research by Mary-Jane Gibson

Manufactured in the United States of America

First American Edition: October 1999
10 9 8 7 6 5 4 3 2 1

contents

introduction

For thousands of years people created altars in their dwellings. The home altar was a sacred space, a visible symbol of the connection between heaven and earth. It brought meaning into ordinary moments of life and served as a focal point for communing with spiritual realms.

Home altars have always been important to me. Even as a child I had an altar. There was a small windowsill next to my bed that I imagined was a special and enchanting place, a place where fairies could meet and dance. As a sort of homage, I placed beautiful things there – my "treasures": bunches of hand-picked flowers, colorful leaves, polished stones, little bits of moss, and bright pieces of broken glass. It was magical.

As part of my spiritual journey as an adult, I have reclaimed the ancient art of the home shrine. Every corner and niche of my home is filled with altars. The objects on these altars are sacred to me; they each represent a hallowed aspect of life. My present-day altars serve as reminders of the profound mysteries of the universe and are places where I feel at peace.

The process of creating this book was a reflection of the material within its pages. It was a moving experience that was filled with remarkable coincidences and synchronicities. For example, I was reading a magazine article about altars when a publisher called and asked me to write this book. Again, when I needed to find a photographer for the book, the first person I contacted was "coincidentally" passionate about altars and had them throughout her house. Additionally, the photographer and I, and our assistants, made extraordinary preparations before each photograph. We meditated in front of every altar before the picture was taken and felt that our meditations and prayers infused each altar with an exhilarating energy that could be felt through the photograph.

Every person who contributed to this book was a loving part of the process. At every juncture, it seemed as if angels, both human and divine, were gently guiding this project toward completion. I have enjoyed writing this book immensely and it is with great joy that I share it with you.

THE *mystery*

Imagine traveling back in time to an ancient land. It is early morning, nearing the time of the summer solstice. A woman stands in her open doorway. Her family is still sleeping. She notices that the sunlight filtering through the trees has created a lovely pattern of shadow and light on the forest floor. Soon her family will awaken and her day will begin. But for now she is alone in the stillness of the new day before she begins to prepare the morning meal.

Stepping inside the house, she goes to the family altar and lights a single candle. The gentle flickering creates wavering shadows throughout the dark room. With deliberate care, she picks up a small figurine from the altar and slowly turns it in her hand. It was a gift from her grandmother. Her fingers mold the curves and crevices of the hardened clay. Carefully she returns the figurine to its place. Closing her eyes, she prays for blessings for her family and gives thanks to the Divine for the good fortune that has already been received. For a moment the room seems to shimmer with tranquility. Calmly opening her eyes she smiles, and snuffs out the candle.

At the beginning of a new day, nearing the time of the solstice, light filtering through the trees inspires a connection to the mysterious forces of the universe.

From these moments spent in reflection, this woman gains the strength she needs for the day. The time that she spends at her home altar nourishes her soul and provides her with the inner wisdom and patience needed for the coming hours. Whether she is making a meal, nursing her baby, or tending the garden, the quiet interval she experiences every morning creates an inner wellspring of serenity that she can tap into whenever she feels the need.

Since time immemorial, the primary function of altars and shrines has been to provide sacred and holy places amid the ordinary reality of life

Since the earliest times, people have created home altars to commune with the Divine and pray for blessings. Altars have been used as a visible symbol of the unity between the Self and the universe – an interface between heaven and earth. Traditionally they have been a place for personal devotions – a place where prayers for fertility, abundant crops, safe return of loved ones and success in daily endeavors were made. Shrines and altars have been used in many ways, but their primary function has been to provide sacred and holy places amid the ordinary reality of life.

The Subliminal Altar

Although the tradition of building altars and shrines still exists in some present-day cultures, most western people grow up without a home altar. However, even during our current period in history, when the mystical side of reality has largely been neglected or ignored, the ancient custom of making home altars has persisted in some interesting, if largely unconscious, forms.

The urge to create sacred spaces is so deep in the human psyche that, even when there is no formalized intent to make an altar, we often create them subconsciously by the way we gather our photos on a piano, or by the way that we carefully arrange objects on a desk or around a computer. This practice of deliberately grouping objects together may indeed be a descendant of the tradition of the home altar. The artful arrangements of books, flowers, candles and objets d'art commonly seen on coffee tables, fireplace mantels, dresser tops and other places throughout many homes and offices are perhaps an outer manifestation of an inner urge to establish hallowed and holy spaces in our environment.

Objects gathered on a dresser by the window and on a side shelf are examples of subliminal altars.

Each item we display in the home, whether or not we realize it, makes a statement about which of our values and family traditions we wish to emphasize in our lives. Carefully placed groups of photos or displays of trinkets, jewelry, books or inherited objects reveal to the observer some of the values which are cherished by the home's occupants. For example, by grouping together old family photos in a niche in the wall, you may be unknowingly creating a memorial or ancestral altar which communicates the message that your family is important to you. A shelf filled with small animal figures might be a subliminal return to the native custom of exhibiting symbols of animal totems on an altar. Clustering special items around a computer

monitor or on a desk can be an unintentional way of establishing an altar. However, because this process of creating an altar is a subconscious one, many of the spiritual benefits derived from the deliberate creation of the home altar are lost.

The value of consciously creating an altar is substantial. It can fill a void in the human psyche that yearns for the mysterious and the wondrous. By reinstating some of the customs from the past that were so sustaining and fulfilling, such as the purposeful creation of home altars (and adapting them to modern use), we welcome mystical and spiritual experiences into our lives.

Why Have an Altar?

Making and using a home altar is a tradition that anyone can follow, regardless of philosophical beliefs, and there is enormous value in returning to this time-honored custom. Present-day home shrines and altars can serve many functions. They not only bring a sense of the sacred into our living spaces, but in a deeper way they can provide a focal point so that we can connect with the spiritual realms within ourselves.

A home altar is like a small temple in your house. It can assist on the journey toward healing and self-integration, and serve as a place to honor celebrations and holidays.

A home altar can assist the journey toward healing and self-integration, and help us find courage to face life's challenges

It can also be used as a centerpoint for honoring rites of passage and life transitions. An altar can help bring a sense of order and meaning to key moments in life, such as births, baptisms, graduations, marriages, career changes, deaths, holidays, the changing of the seasons and other important turning points.

Creating a home altar can help strengthen family relationships. It is through initiating the process of remembering our connection to the sacred whole, to those who came before us as well as to those who will follow, that we can find the courage and human resources necessary to face the problems of the future. An altar can assist this process and encourage an ongoing sense of continuity by being a place to honor past, present and future family members.

The home altar can also be used as a site for celebration and manifestation. Adorning an altar with fresh flowers, ripe fruit, aromatic candles and special objects creates a wonderful metaphor for joy and happiness. To understand the potential power of altars in modern life, it helps if you understand the ancient traditions upon which they stand.

Altars Throughout History

The yearning to create sacred places may be a part of our spiritual inheritance. Perhaps, deep within the psyche of humanity, the voices of our ancestors resound, such that each of us has a subconscious remembrance of the power of ancient rites at hallowed altars. Conceivably, residing in the collective unconscious within us is the memory of those primitive altars which can be traced back thousands of years to pre-human times.

The oldest known altars in the world were made by Neanderthal people in caves high up in the Alps approximately 75,000 years ago. These caves, excavated in the early 1900s, revealed altars made for rituals celebrating the Paleolithic cult of the bear. Researchers discovered carefully arranged cave bear skulls and bones. Some of the skulls had rings of stones placed around them, while other ceremonial arrangements were created from various combinations of cave bear bones.[1] Ancient home altars from the Neolithic period were also excavated from sites at Çatal Hüyük and Hacilar in Turkey that date back to between 8000 and 6000 BC.[2]

Home altars have been found throughout history. In both the West African and ancient Nordic religions, altars were thought to symbolize the "throne of a god" and were made of a large stone or a heap of stones. In Hindu tradition, altars were considered to be places where the gods were invited or summoned. Some early cultures used burial mounds as altars, and it is presumed that these practices symbolized death leading to life and rebirth. In other traditions fire altars were used to represent this cyclical link between life and death, because fire can die down and then rise up again.[3]

The word "altar" is derived from a Latin word meaning a high place. Early personal altars were often elevated on platforms, tables, or hilltops. These lofty altars were where celestial beings were honored. Occasionally, however, altars were placed in low areas, such as in fireplaces and excavated pits. The hearth, which was under the domain of the Roman goddess Vesta (known as Hestia to the Greeks), was considered to be one prototype of the low altar. [4]

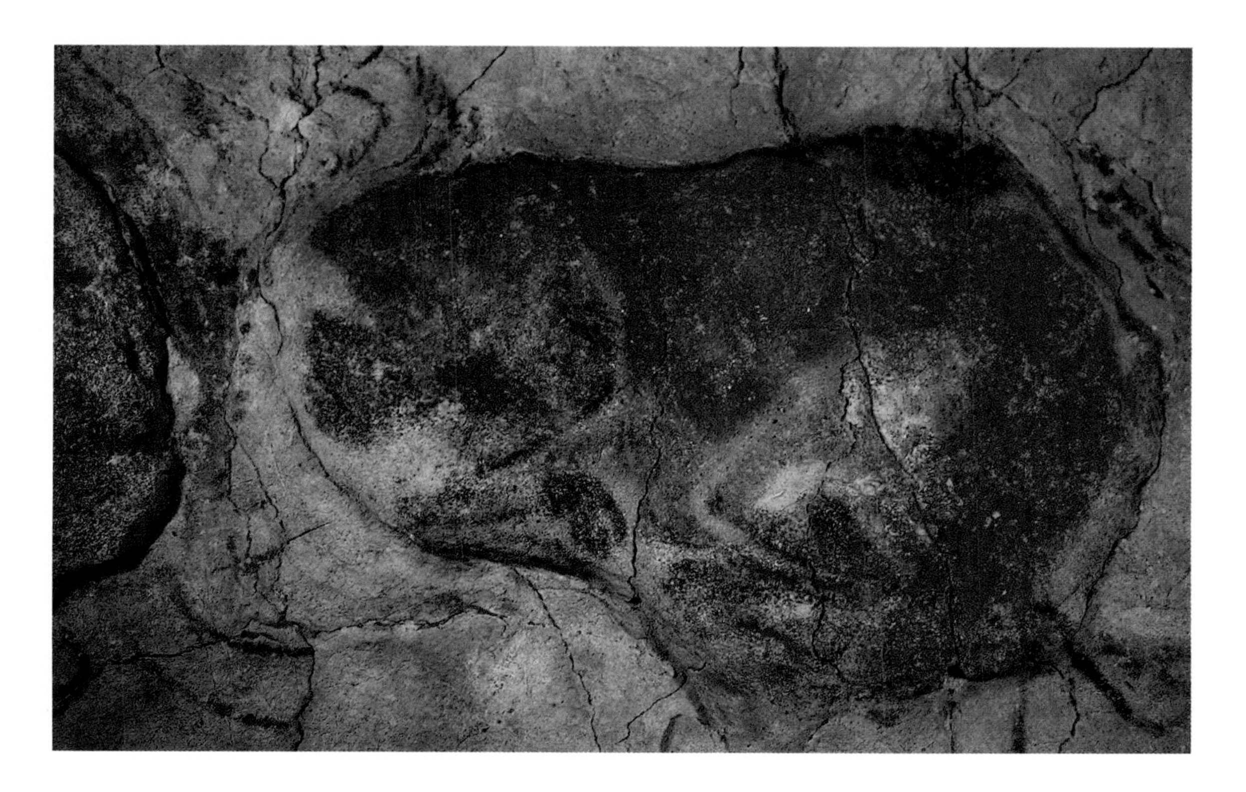

Ancient cave drawings were used as focal points for worship and communing with the unseen world.

1 Campbell, Joseph, *The Masks of God: Primitive Mythology,* New York: The Viking Press, 1959, pp. 339-42.

2 Turner, Kay, "Why we are so inclined...", *Lady-Unique-Inclination-of-the-Night, Cycle 6,* Spring 1983, p. 5.

3 Bolle, K.W., "Altar: Historical Background," *New Catholic Encyclopedia,* Vol. A, New York: McGraw Hill and Co., 1967, p. 343.

4 Ibid.

Many ancient shrines and altars have survived the destructive forces of time. Some of the world's most breathtaking art and architecture has been used to house these shrines and altars, and they often serve as sites for pilgrimages. From the lofty Xisnfeng (Fairy Summit) Temple on a sacred mountain in China, to the altars in the Great Pyramids of Egypt and at Newgrange in Ireland, altars and shrines throughout the world continue to speak to us of the majesty of Spirit (the Creator). One way to touch the power of these places is to embark upon a pilgrimage. By tracing the pathways of previous generations and by viewing the shrine through their eyes, you are reestablishing a time-honored custom. Often the spiritual energy surrounding ancient altars and shrines continues to radiate for centuries after their construction. Similarly, you can imbue your home with the grace of these sacred places by learning about altars and understanding their underlying principles.

Why Altars Work

In many ways the power of the altar lies in its visible appearance. The structure and objects of the altar appeal to our psyche because they give form to the formless and provide a visual representation of the Divine. It is difficult to comprehend the spiritual realm because of its unseeable nature. However, when objects are thoughtfully placed on an altar, they physically represent things which by their very essence are invisible, thus giving substance to faith.[5]

Just looking at an altar can influence the way that you are feeling. You may be conscious of the pleasing colors, pleasant smells and beautiful images, and this can have an effect on you. However, in a much deeper sense, it is the subconscious mind, which is the part of the brain that dictates our beliefs, that becomes profoundly imprinted with the symbolic meanings of the objects on an altar. The subconscious mind has much more influence on your life than your conscious mind. It determines your deepest passions about life and even influences your destiny.

The altar objects exert a powerful influence on the subconscious because they simultaneously express various levels of truth beyond the reality of surface appearances, thus helping to create understanding out of the complexities of life.[6] Altar items are physical objects, yet each one represents an ideal, belief, relationship, concept or idea. Together these objects become not separate symbols, but a synthesis that is far more than the sum of its parts. It is an altar's coherent and whole gestalt that so effectively impacts the subconscious mind.

The various components of the altar are not usually considered to be idols commanding worship, but rather reflections of the spiritual side of our lives. For example, a rose on a home altar might represent love. In some cultures, however, symbolic objects and representations are taken literally. In the ancient Hindu tradition, for example, objects representing the gods were not considered to be

Previous pages: sunrise at the prehistoric stone circle at Avebury, England – a shrine for sacred ritual.

5 Turner, p. 7

6 Torre, Susan, as quoted by Turner, p. 11.

merely symbolic. When people encountered such an object, they believed that they were actually in the presence of the divinity so represented and would, therefore, be in a position to receive blessings from the god or goddess.[7] While most people today do not share this literal view, nonetheless symbolic objects play a very important role in shaping our beliefs, which in turn can greatly determine the reality of life as we experience it. All the objects on an altar work as catalysts for the inner knowing places within us.

The simple ritual of lighting a candle at an altar can infuse ordinary moments with sacred meaning

The visible form of an altar can also help strengthen our connection to our past and our future. This can occur through the use of ceremony which accompanies the use of altars. Whether the ritual used is thousands of years old, or whether it is a simple act like lighting a candle, ritual and ceremony are filled with the substance of life and carry us to the essence of being.

Most of our ancestors utilized ceremonial practices in every aspect of their lives, honoring the milestones in life, from birth to death. These rituals, performed solemnly in front of an altar, reinforced the fact that an individual was not alone but rather an integral part of a larger community which extended both backward and forward in time. Using the objects on the altar as focal points for ceremony helped put ordinary experiences into perspective within the greater panorama of life, and provided a way to step out of ordinary reality into sacred and spiritual realms.

Altars and the Connection to Spirit

In the fast pace of today's world there is a growing need to reconnect to the sacred elements of life. An altar can fulfill this need through being a powerful visible representation of the spiritual energy that surrounds and sustains us. It serves as a kind of reminder of our connection to spiritual realms. Creating and using an altar can be an effective means of forging a connection to higher powers. A home shrine can be a gateway between the seen and unseen realms which can connect us to the rhythms of nature and the universe. This can help infuse the most ordinary aspects of life with a divine sense of meaning. The physical form of an altar reminds us of the importance of honoring the hallowed places within ourselves; it is also a focus for prayers to the spiritual forces that shape our lives.

An altar dedicated to increasing your spiritual awareness can become an energetic point of convergence for symbols that propel the human spirit forward. It can bring a remarkable grace and beauty into your life. This type of altar can be used in three ways. It can be used as a place to pray and ask for divine guidance, a place to listen to messages from the spiritual realm and a place to give thanks for blessings received.

7 Mutén, Burleigh, Ed., *Return of the Great Goddess,* Boston: Shambhala, 1994, p. 3.

Prayer and Devotion

The ancient and universal function of altars as places of worship and devotion can offer a much-needed dimension to modern life regardless of religious affiliation. It can help refuel spiritual reserves by linking personal hopes and beliefs to a higher context. Using a home altar for prayers can help instill a feeling that we are not alone; it can function as a reminder that there are beings in the realm of spirit close by, waiting to assist us. In this way the altar serves as it did in former times, evoking in us the awareness that the prosaic reality of everyday life is actually filled with wonder and magic. It can be a great comfort knowing that we don't have to do it all alone – we don't have to make every life decision on our own – because there are loving spiritual beings waiting to guide and protect us. This can provide the courage we need to face obstacles which might otherwise seem too daunting to confront and overcome.

Listening

The altar is not only a place of supplication and prayer; it is also a place for listening to our own intuition. The art of listening can be as profound as worship. An altar can provide a visible focus point where you can quiet your thoughts and listen to messages from your own inner knowing as well as from the spiritual realm. When we think of asking for help from the Creator in our lives, we sometimes forget that an important part of prayer is just being still and listening for answers. The altar is an excellent place to tune in to the messages which are sent to us. Sometimes we pray for answers and help, and then, when they are sent, we are too busy to notice. Taking the time simply to wait with an attitude of receptivity is one of the most direct and powerful ways we can connect to the Divine and receive the answers we seek. An altar can provide a valuable and sacred place to do this.

An altar is a sacred place for praying, listening to divine guidance and giving thanks for blessings

Giving Thanks

Another important function of the personal Spirit Altar is that it gives us a place where we can go to give thanks. Prayers of gratitude were among the most common and central functions of ancient altars. Appreciation for the bounty and blessings in life is one of the most effective ways of increasing these qualities. Being grateful for the goodness in your life creates a kind of magnetic attraction for even more blessings to come your way. Gratitude helps you be receptive to the life force of the universe.

Previous pages and right: This Home Altar is dedicated to Mother Mary and Jesus, and is adorned with salt, bread, wine and candles.

Placing on an altar symbols that represent things for which you are appreciative increases your connection to the spiritual realm. The more thankful you are to the Creator, the more you will have to be thankful for. The altar reminds us of this truth. If you don't express your gratitude, you lessen your life force. Being appreciative empowers and strengthens you, and an altar can help crystallize your thoughts toward gratitude, thus connecting you more deeply to spirit.

Altars for Personal Integration

In modern life we tend to have many different roles. We may look like one person on the outside, but we often have a number of sub-personalities within. Sometimes these different aspects of self pull us in so many different directions that we lose a sense of who we really are.

You can use your altar to combat this tendency by placing objects on it that symbolically characterize various aspects of your life, and are arranged in a pleasing combination. In this way, an altar can serve as a kind of microcosmic representation of your life, where the arrangement of the altar objects can serve as a metaphor for integration and harmony. For example, a paintbrush on an altar might depict an artistic part of you, a small silver spoon might represent the mothering part of you and a gold fountain pen might represent your career. Putting them together on an altar can be a powerful metaphor for those three aspects of yourself being in harmony with each other rather than at odds. An altar used in this way can be a place where you can symbolically bring together the various disparate elements of your life, so they can be welded together into a unified, coherent whole.

Clustering objects on your altar that represent aspects of yourself can help you to step beyond fragmentation into the larger scheme of life. By arranging and rearranging the elements on your altar, you can symbolically reorder your life. The human psyche responds to symbolic acts, and when you use your home altar as a template for personal cohesion, it becomes a centralized point for inner synthesis.[8]

An Integration Altar can also help deepen your connection to Spirit by the placement of objects that represent parts of yourself next to others that represent spiritual realms. This can subliminally intensify your link to the Creator. Feelings of meaninglessness and of being pulled in too many directions are often soothed and healed. The Integration Altar can be a peaceful center in the busy whirl of life, a place where we can go to regain a sense of wholeness and unity.

Art supplies arranged on one part of an altar symbolize integrating art and creativity into ordinary life.

8 Turner, p. 7.

Pumpkin
BURPEE
MAMMOTH
SUNFLOWER
Fun Seeds
Bachelor Button
Spray 'nGlue
Damar Varnish
KRYLON
RUBBER CEMENT
Utrecht
Utrecht
Utrecht

Altars for Healing

Altars have been used for healing since earliest times. Today, they can provide a powerful focus for sending healing energy to yourself and others, and they can also be a distillation point to receive vital nurturing energies from Spirit. There is increasing scientific support for what ancient healers have always known – that the body, mind (including your emotions) and soul are not separate. The altar is a place where body, mind and soul can be healed. (See The Healing Altar, pages 36–39.)

Life Transitions and the Home Altar

Traditionally an altar was also used as a place to memorialize the turning points in life. This type of altar is valuable in today's world because there is a noticeable lack of places where we can express and celebrate life experiences. In ancient times, whether the events were happy or sad, there were always appropriate rituals for commemorating significant losses and major successes. By contrast, in modern life, a person is often given only one day off work to attend the funeral of a family member, and few people acknowledge that the period of mourning extends far beyond the funeral. The end of a marriage is often marked only by the ceremony of signing legal papers and perhaps an appearance in court. To honor happier occasions, we may go out with friends to celebrate a new job or moving to a new home. But often these festivities consist of little more than a round of drinks or possibly dinner, while the deeper personal significance of what has taken place may be overlooked.

The home altar is a place where life's passages can be given their proper homage over a longer period of time through the use of ritual and ceremony. This can help you process, acknowledge and fully experience each of the important events in your life. When you use an altar to honor the transitions in your life, you are taking the feelings that are inside you and giving them a physical form. This articulation gives your emotions the attention and care that they deserve, and allows you truly to hear what is in your heart.

Altars and the Continuity of Life

Today we have forgotten the tribal awareness that life flows behind us and unfolds before us. We have lost the sense of continuity of life – the understanding that we are a new sprout from an ancient root. In the past, home altars were used as a place to honor ancestors, strengthen relationships between family members and send love to descendants. The Ancestral Altar served as a visible reminder that we stand on the shoulders of our ancestors, and it created a feeling of being a part of a continuum.

In the present world, a home altar can be used to help reconnect with our distant past and remember our connection to the sacred whole – to those who came before us as well as those who will follow. An altar can be a wonderful repository for memories, both personal and cultural. It can also be a place where we can honor our relatives and our heroes. It can contain visual representations of the people we love, both living and dead. The altar offers us a place and a means of symbolically honoring our connection to our past and our present, our hopes for our children and our feelings about those who may no longer be in our lives. It is through initiating this process of remembering that we are each part of the greater human family that we can find the courage and human resources necessary to face the problems of the future.

Altars for Manifestation

A home altar can help you achieve your life goals. It is a place where you can sit in stillness to sort through your values and desires, and get to the heart of what it is you really want in your life. When you gain clarity regarding your hopes and dreams, it becomes much easier to manifest or create them. In addition, if you choose objects for your altar that symbolize your desires and place them next to objects that denote the spiritual realms, your altar becomes a sacred template that can enable you to achieve your goals in accordance with your highest good.

A home altar becomes a spiritual oasis where the important aspects of your life come into focus

As you spend time at your altar, you may find that many unexpected and happy coincidences begin to occur in your life, even if you have not consciously been looking for them. This occurs because when you create your altar and meditate there on a regular basis, you create a gathering point for positive energy. This energy is often subconsciously directed toward areas of your life where you need to make changes or where you want to achieve results.

Altars and Transcendence

Creating and using an altar can be an extraordinary process. Every step of your home altar – deciding its purpose, assembling the objects for it, constructing it and finally using it – can be a transformational and transcending experience. Transcendence is the ability to begin anew, to enter into a state of grace, with the awareness that, no matter what your past has been, right now you are creating a new beginning. A home altar can transport you into this state of transcendence where you can clarify what is important in your life, connect with the creative forces of the universe and truly begin anew. It is a sacred space in your home that continually projects a radiant energy and is a constant reminder of the greater realms of spirit within and around us.

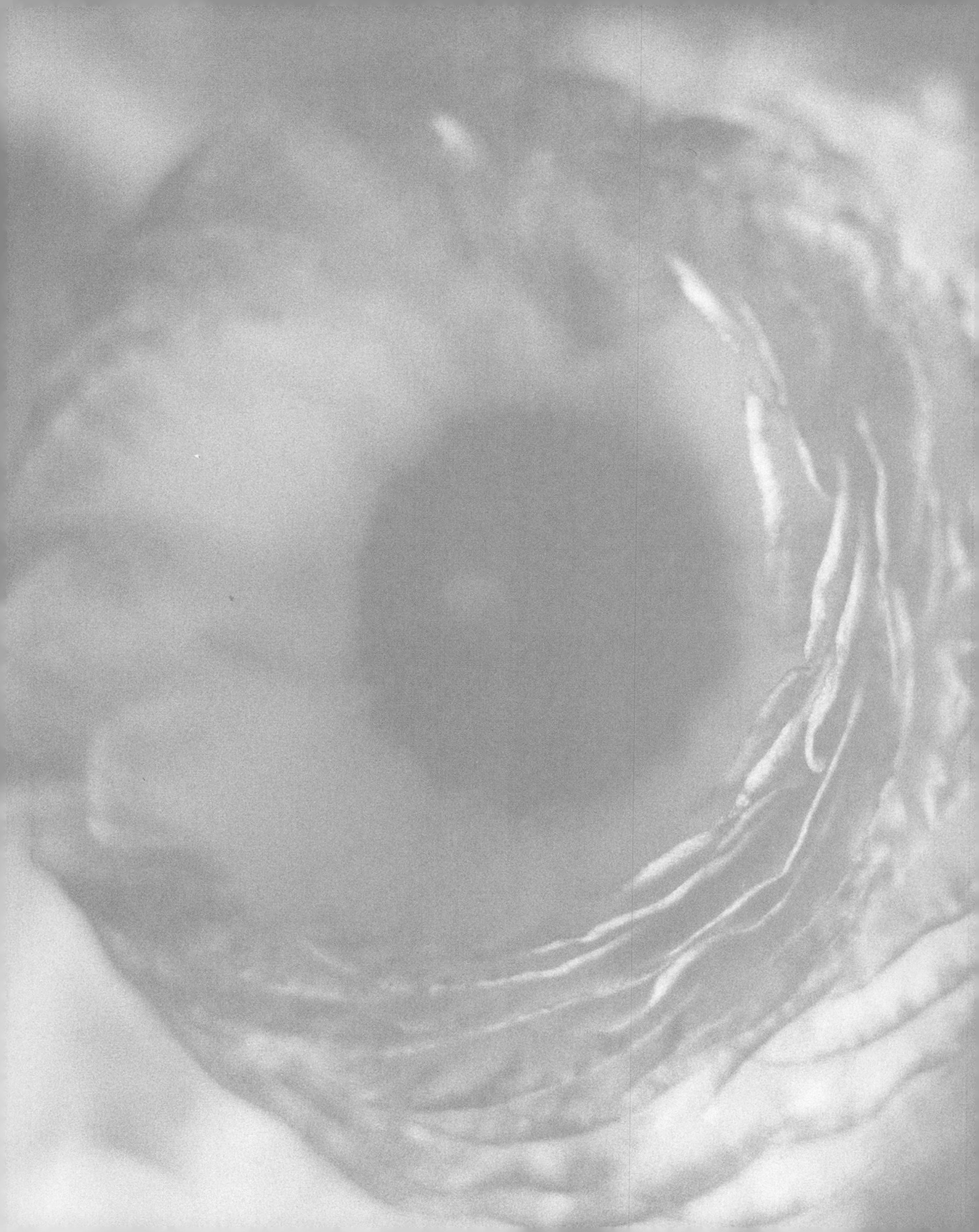

THE *spirit*

THE *Spirit Altar*

Your altar is a focal point for the sacred: a place where you can retreat for stillness and reflection. It can serve as an anchor through difficult times as well as be a place to celebrate when you feel on top of the world. Your personal shrine can also be where the various and sometimes conflicting facets of life can be symbolically joined together in a meaningful and deeply satisfying way. There is no limit to the kinds of altars which can be created. Some people decide to have one main altar, which may change over time as different needs or occasions arise. Others choose to create a special altar with one particular focus. Some individuals construct a multi-purpose altar that combines a variety of themes. Whatever yearning you hold in your heart, whatever you hope for and dream of – these will serve as guides for deciding how you want to use your altar.

One of the most profound uses of an altar is as a sacred place to deepen your connection with the Divine. This type of altar serves as a bridge between the reality of everyday life and spiritual realms. It is a place of prayer where you can untangle the brambles of your mind, quiet your thoughts and listen to messages from the Creator. It is a holy space that can call you back to your true nature.

A Spirit Altar deepens your connections to the Divine, and helps you find an inner balance

The creation of a Spirit Altar mirrors the intent of its form. Each step of the process needs to be infused with energy, care and mindfulness. Go slowly and make sure everything feels right before proceeding with the next step. Every altar item should be chosen carefully, bearing in mind its significance and power. There is no prescribed way to make this type of altar; rather it is the love and the clarity of your intent that makes it hallowed.

A Spirit Altar should have three components. There should be something on the altar that signifies the Divine, something that signifies you or humans in general and something that represents the gateway or doorway between the two realms. A very simple example of this might be including a feather to represent the heavens, a stone to represent the earth and humans, and a candle to represent the transcendental doorway between the two realms. Using the three components, the Spirit Altar thus becomes a place to affirm your unity with the cosmos and to find an inner balance and harmony. It becomes a distillation point through which the creative forces of the universe can flow to you.

Flowers, fruit and candles adorn this Zen Altar – creating a focal point for daily meditation.

THE DIVINE *Feminine Altar*

A particular kind of Spirit Altar is the Divine Feminine Altar. These altars date back to the earliest times. The first altars were thought to symbolize Mother Earth's regenerative womb. In ancient times the words "home," "womb," "woman," "vessel," "temple" and "altar" were synonymous. Goddess shrines and altars were found everywhere – by the threshold, near the hearth, in a sacred grove of trees, by the well. The Goddess represented wisdom, compassion and the life-force in all things, and women were the first custodians of these shrines. The home altar was the place where a woman could ignite these mysterious and wondrous forces of the Divine Feminine principle for the benefit of herself and her family.

You can bring the Goddess qualities into your life by creating an altar dedicated to this purpose. On your altar you might consider placing a Goddess figurine – reproductions are quite easy to obtain. Original figurines date back to 30,000 BC and were found all across Europe, from Siberia to the Ukraine. They were sculpted in bone, stone, clay and coal, and had large fully shaped breasts, bellies and buttocks, representing fertile potential. You also might consider placing a bowl, basket, cauldron or chalice on your altar to symbolize the receptive energy of the feminine spirit.

When you begin to use your Divine Feminine Altar it is almost as if, magically, the creative forces of the universe take you under their wing and gradually allow you to soar into vast inner spaces of your being.

Previous pages and left: Goddess Altars with figurines representing the Divine Feminine spirit. In the foreground, the "circle of friends" creates a community altar.

THE *Healing Altar*

Throughout history, Healing Altars have been used to invoke life-giving energies. Whenever you create and use a Healing Altar, you are entering into a time-honored tradition which can help you move toward physical, emotional and spiritual healing. Your Healing Altar can also be a focal point where you can concentrate and focus healing energies on others.

Altar Objects for a Healing Altar

A Healing Altar should always be sparkling clean. Don't allow a layer of dust to accumulate. The objects should be cleaned or cleansed periodically. Make sure that the colors on the altar and the altar cloth (if you are using one) are clean and bright rather than murky and muddy. Every aspect of the altar should sing with vibrant light and energy.

On a Healing Altar you might want to include an object that represents the person you want to heal, such as a photograph or drawing of the individual. If your altar is dedicated to self-healing, then you should use a photo of yourself. Make sure that any photo you place on a Healing Altar exemplifies good physical and emotional health, and does not show an unhappy or unhealthy-looking person. If your altar is dedicated to global healing, then you might want to place a small globe or a picture of the earth on the altar.

A symbol of the spiritual realms in the center of your altar is a reminder that inner guidance is never far away

It is also essential to place something that symbolizes the spiritual realms in the center of the altar. This is important. It provides a subliminal reminder that you are not alone in your journey to wholeness; spiritual help is always near.

Some of the objects on your Healing Altar should be metaphors for the type of healing you hope to achieve. For example, if your altar is dedicated to physical healing, there should be objects on it that are metaphors for excellent health, such as a vigorous plant or a photograph of a physical activity, such as river rafting, jogging or mountain climbing. If your altar is dedicated to healing emotional wounds, use objects that are metaphors for this. For instance, one woman used thin silver wire to wrap around and connect the broken pieces of a glass heart back together. She

A Healing Altar dedicated to emotional healing and inner peace. The central Kwan Yin figurine represents divine compassion and serenity.

said she was creating a symbol for the healing of her broken heart.

To increase the energy field around your Healing Altar you might consider placing a quartz crystal on its surface. Crystals have been used for healing purposes since the earliest times and are excellent on an altar dedicated to healing. To increase a crystal's healing qualities, first cleanse it by rubbing it with eucalyptus oil, or by soaking it in salt water, or by leaving it out in the sun for at least five hours. Then hold the crystal next to your heart and say, "I dedicate this stone to healing. May this stone receive and radiate light and love." Carefully place the crystal on your altar, where its presence will continue to magnify and expand the altar's healing energy.

Emotional Healing

In ancient cultures ceremony and ritual were used to aid the grieving process and to help remedy emotional or behavioral imbalances. The structure of the ceremony provided a form for the emerging emotions to be released constructively. In present times, an altar can give a focus point that can help anchor you on your journey to emotional wholeness.

Healing grief, sadness and the loss of a loved one are areas that an altar can help. Some kinds of grief, which might be difficult to discuss casually, can be privately processed and mourned at an altar. One example of this is the death of a pet. The loss of a pet is sometimes passed off as a minor event, but for many it can mean the loss of a companion who was loved for many years. Placing objects representing this loss on your altar, such as a loved photograph of your pet or a favorite toy, and spending time at your altar remembering the good times that were shared, can be a way of honoring the pain and beginning to heal the sorrow.

A Healing Altar can also be of assistance in the healing of the wound of raw anger in response to a grievance. Sometimes angry emotions can be too intense to be controlled and they can escalate unless we find a suitable way of processing them. Using an altar as a place to perform healing ceremonies can provide a safe means of releasing these intense emotions. For

A shell used on an emotional Healing Altar can represent an acceptance of the ebbing and flowing of emotions.

example, a woman arrived home angry every day because of inconsiderate drivers that she encountered on her drive from work. To begin to heal this anger she used one of her son's toy cars and placed it on the altar to represent her on her afternoon drive. Next to the car she placed an exquisite figurine of a white dove which she thought epitomized peace and serenity. (A powerful metaphor is created when objects which represent a problem are placed next to objects that represent Spirit.)

Every morning before work she sat in contemplation before her altar and affirmed to herself, "I am a balanced and peaceful woman." She reported that she felt much more peaceful when driving after she began using her altar in this way. Her altar helped her to form a template in her mind for calmness which helped influence her reaction to the events around her.

One way to use your altar for emotional healing is to write on a piece of paper the name of the emotion or behavior that you wish to release. Stand before your altar and burn the paper, holding the intention that you will heal this aspect of your life. Keep the ashes in a small container on your altar as a reminder of the release of the behavior. By creating and using a Healing Altar in subtle ways, the mind is gently influenced toward inward healing. The altar becomes a special place where the body, mind and soul can truly be healed.

At a Healing Altar, emotional imbalances can be improved and body, mind and soul made whole

Healing Altar in a Hospital

Creating a Healing Altar in a hospital room can offer great solace to someone who is ill. You can easily create this type of altar by throwing a scarf over the top of a dresser, windowsill, shelf or hospital bedside table. Then simply place a few very special items on its surface, including one object that represents excellent health and another that represents Spirit. An altar can instantly shift the energy in a hospital room from sterile and cold to warm and healing.

THE *Manifestation Altar*

Your home altar can be an important tool for manifestation and for making your dreams come true. It can act as a catalyst to activate your inner forces for creating what you desire. There are as many kinds of Manifestation Altars as there are personal visions. The following altars can be adapted to suit your personal needs.

The Love Altar

Creating an altar to bring more love into your life can be a joyous and fulfilling activity. It can also help you gain a perspective and understanding of the love that currently exists in your life, as well as draw more love to you in the future. When you are creating your Love Altar, remember that all love is an expression of our union with Spirit. Sometimes it is easy to get stuck on one aspect of love and to forget that true love is really a deepening of the connection to yourself, others and the Creator. Whether you want to find your soul mate, increase the love in your family or fill your heart with love for all humanity or your bed with more passion, the Love Altar begins with a connection to the creative loving force in the universe.

Begin your Love Altar by finding a representation of what divine love means to you. This object or picture can serve as a reminder that your higher power always wants you to have and to give love. This realization is the cornerstone of bringing more love into your life. Next fill your altar with whatever images, fabrics, natural objects, jewels, flowers, scents or colors symbolize the love that you want to manifest. Rich velvets in shades of purple and red, gauzy silk, dried rose petals, fresh flowers, the scent of musk, rose quartz crystals, photos of loved ones past and present – all these can stimulate the love centers in your heart and mind. As you meditate on them, they will put you in a loving frame of mind which will naturally attract more love into your life.

If you desire romantic love in your life, put pairs of things on your altar to symbolize a couple, such as a pair of lovebird figurines. Do not put a photo of yourself alone, as this is not a good metaphor for the future. Other items you can place on your Love Altar are statues or pictures of embracing couples, statuettes of Venus, Aphrodite or Cupid, incense such as ylang ylang (which is associated with romantic love), or pink candles.

This Love Altar includes symbols of love. The angel represents the higher power of love.

The Abundance Altar

Abundance is a concept which exists in the mind as much as in the physical world. There are individuals who, by many standards, are considered rich. And yet these people worry about their assets and fret each day about losing the wealth that they already have. At the other end of the spectrum are people who have little material wealth beyond food and shelter but who count themselves truly rich because they love their work, have happy children or have other similar, priceless treasures for which they are thankful.

The first step in creating your Abundance Altar is to evaluate what wealth, abundance and prosperity mean to you. Sometimes people believe themselves to be poor only because they have failed to take stock of the many wonderful things they already have. The phenomenon of abundance is closely tied to the principle of gratitude. The more thankful you are for what you have, the more wealth is attracted to you. When assembling your Abundance Altar, it is valuable to include some symbolic elements that represent what you already enjoy in life.

In a spirit of gratitude, take time to make an inventory of the good things in your life. When you have finished, decide what additional things you need or desire to feel abundant. Does being prosperous mean having more time to do things you love? Having more furniture? Or having the means to travel to exotic places? What makes one person feel affluent might mean something completely different to someone else.

Golden bags of grain, a gilded Buddha and a bowl of rice adorn this Abundance Altar. A crystal bottle (right) might also be appropriate for an Abundance altar.

A terrapin on an Abundance Altar can represent stability and groundedness.

One man might feel incredibly wealthy because his job as a photojournalist allows him to travel all around the world. To another person, the incredibly long hours that this man has to work, as well as all the time he spends away from home, might seem like a very poor life. This second person's idea of wealth might be a small secluded cabin in the woods where she could be free from the hustle and bustle of modern life. Take time to visualize clearly whatever images come up for you around words like luxury, abundance and wealth. The pictures and sensations which fill your mind will guide you in the selection of objects for your Abundance Altar. Make sure that when the objects are assembled, your altar feels abundant. For one person the color gold and richly patterned fabrics, beautiful stones, rich scents and heavy, embossed picture frames might be associated with luxury, so these would be good for her Abundance Altar. For another person, photos of exotic beaches might generate a feeling of affluence. Let your altar be a template for the prosperity that you desire and you may find abundance filling your life.

The Fertility Altar

Fertility Altars are among the most traditional and ancient kinds of altars. Celebrating the fecundity of our human bodies is a way of affirming all life and continuance of our planet, even if you are not actively seeking to conceive a child. Fertility Altars can be used for affirming a highly productive,

Fruit, rice, a lingam stone and a figurine of a goddess with ample breasts are symbols of fecundity that you could place on your Fertility Altar.

prolific or fruitful time in your life. They can also be used to activate the Divine Feminine energy which dwells within you and all people.

However, if you are trying to become pregnant, creating a Fertility Altar is a very special and conscious way to begin the life of a new being. The energy which you put into this process will ensure that your child will feel your desire and love even before it is conceived. What a wonderful way to come into the world – into a family which has created a special and sacred altar dedicated to a much-wanted child!

On your Fertility Altar you might consider using reproductions of ancient fertility symbols, such as clay goddesses with voluptuous hips and breasts. Some of these figures depict women giving birth or nursing infants. These ancient symbols of the Earth Mother are compelling in their portrayal of the process of rejuvenation and renewal. Including these on a Fertility Altar creates an immediate tie to goddess energies.

Other objects and symbols which are excellent for Fertility Altars are carved and colored eggs made out of polished stone or wood. Eggs are often used to symbolize fertility. Representations of fresh new growth and the colors of springtime are also associated with fertility and new birth. Pictures of babies, mothers, young animals, the abundance of the earth, new grass and the buds of flowers – all these images call forth within you the forces of new life, of beginnings and of fertility.

Celebrate and generate fruitfulness and productivity in all aspects of your life at a Fertility Altar

For your Fertility Altar you may also want to include fertility symbols from the past. In old European folklore the bear was associated with motherhood. (Marija Gimbutas discusses this in her book *The Language of the Goddess*.) Along with the deer and the elk-doe, the bear was related to birth and the bearing of children. The root of the Germanic word for "bear" means to bear children. Among the myths of the ancient Greeks and the ancient Sumerians, and also in Scottish and Irish fairy tales, deer are associated with motherhood and life-giving. There is archaeological evidence of a deer cult among prehistoric peoples 14,000 years ago who worshipped the deer as a deity with birth-giving powers. Using representations of these animals on your Fertility Altar is a potent way of energizing the forces of fertility in your consciousness and life.

Deer have an ancient association with regeneration.

An open flower with stamens representing fertility.

The Courage and Faith Altar

There are times in every life which call for courage and exceptional strength and faith. Everyone goes through times of difficulty which can test their ability to hold on through pain and loss and other personal trials. In these times, it can be very comforting to create an altar devoted to courage, strength and faith.

When creating your Courage Altar, include a symbol of strength as one of the focal points. The object may be different for each individual. For people who have a strong religious affiliation, it can be helpful to use icons or photos or small statues of deities and saints, Buddhas or religious teachers. For others, totem animals or objects representing universal symbols of strength, such as mountains, oceans or the cosmos, can feel fortifying. You can include symbols of the earth, which has endured for so many millions of years, and of creatures which are traditionally associated with strength, such as lions, whales and elk. Wooden objects are also good, especially hand-carved ones, which are symbolic of the strength of the trees from which they originated, as well as the patience and strength of the worker who brought the object out of the wood. Altar cloths for this type of home shrine can be made of sturdy fabric, such as homespun linen or wool, which can radiate a feeling of strength. Choose objects that make you feel stronger just by looking at them.

In your contemplation time at your Courage Altar, let the power of the objects you have chosen sink into your awareness. Allow them to become one with you and know that their symbolic strength and endurance are becoming a part of your consciousness. Know that your faith, represented by the special symbols you may have chosen, is lending you energy and strength, so you can face whatever is confronting you at this time in your life. If you have chosen representations of animals for your Courage Altar, such as the elk or tiger, imagine their valor becoming your valor. Know that you will not be given situations which you cannot find the courage to face and move through. Let the energy of faith and courage and strength, which is represented by your altar, flow through your body and soul, making you ready to handle whatever needs to be faced and overcome in your life.

The Creativity Altar

One of the most exhilarating and stimulating processes is the creation of an altar or a sacred place in your home devoted to creativity. Joseph Campbell in *The Power of Myth* said of creating a sacred place in the home, "This is a place where you can simply experience and bring forth what you are and what you might be. This is the place of creative incubation. At first you may find nothing happens there. But if you have a sacred place and use it, something will eventually happen." Creativity is the heart and soul, the very essence of Spirit. It has been said that we are closest to Divine Spirit when we are creative. The possibilities for joyful self-expression are limitless when creating this type of altar.

Cucumber
Pumpkin
MAMMOTH
Bachelor Button
Radish
Damar Varnish
RUBBER CEMENT
Utrecht

What do you want to create? Have you always wanted to try painting, writing, sewing, carpentry, pottery or a new expression of fashion? Don't be limited by traditional ideas about what is within the field of creative endeavor and what is not. Creativity is a kind of attitude which can infuse any human activity with the spark of the Divine. It can turn a dull job into a fulfilling one.

A Creativity Altar can be devoted to a single endeavor or project, or it can be focused on bringing the spirit of creativity into all aspects of your life. When designing your Creativity Altar, let the child inside you come out and play. Don't censor yourself. This altar can be filled with children's toys and memories, as well as more exalted representations of artistic endeavors. Use color, bright and bold. Let yourself fly free and design it any way you want to. Don't be afraid to express yourself and tell your hidden dreams here. No one has to see this but you, if that is the way you want it to be, so go ahead and let go. This is a safe place for uninhibited expression, for trying out the ideas of which you have only dreamed.

The Creativity Altar can also be a place where you symbolically resolve blocks which have prevented you from fully realizing your creative powers. To use your altar in this way, find objects which represent the fulfillment of an unachieved dream. For example, perhaps your parents told you that you were clumsy and you'd never be able to be a good dancer, and yet your creative spirit yearns to dance wild and free. You might find a picture of a dancer or a well-used pair of dance shoes to place on your altar. By physically placing these objects on your home shrine, you allow them to represent the attainment of dreams. Your altar then becomes a template for you to begin to express yourself more creatively. Remember that the longings of your heart are often your higher self asking to be born. The fact that you want to accomplish something is evidence that spirit is leading you in that direction.

An altar dedicated to developing childlike, spontaneous expressions of joy and creativity.

The Affirmation Altar

An Affirmation Altar is somewhat like the Creativity Altar, but it can also address specific areas of your life which may not be directly related to creative endeavors. This type of altar can help you through a difficult time or can assist you to accomplish a specific goal. An Affirmation Altar provides visible symbols for whatever you want to affirm or achieve in your life.

For example, one woman created an Affirmation Altar dedicated to helping her accept her body. Although many people had told her that she was pretty, she always found faults with herself and was unhappy with her voluptuous figure. One day she decided that she wanted to feel differently about this, and so she created an Affirmation Altar to affirm more love for her body.

She found pictures of herself as a young child, as well as other photos picturing her adult self at key points in her life where she felt proud of what she had accomplished. She put these in beautiful unique frames and surrounded them with flowers, polished stones, glass bottles and other objects which she loved and admired. She then carefully lettered affirmations about herself on pieces of handmade paper and arranged these among the other objects and photos on the altar.

One of her calligraphied affirmations read, "I am a vibrant, elegant and attractive woman. I love myself and my body exactly as I am. So be it." During her times of meditation, she would read each affirmation and then carefully place it among the lovely things on the altar. Over time, she began to associate the beauty of the altar with the pictures of herself, and a life-long dislike of her appearance began to melt at first into acceptance, and later into positive feelings about her physical self.

Your Affirmation Altar can help you achieve your goals and dreams

The Affirmation Altar can be devoted to any goal, hope or problem that you want to address. This altar can be very effective in helping you to realize the goals that you have for transforming yourself and your reality. Be sure to state your affirmations as though they have already become real. This prepares your mind to grow into this new awareness. Find objects and pictures, textures, colors and scents which symbolically correspond to the situation or attitudes which you want to change. Meditate in the presence of these things, saying aloud the affirmations which you have chosen for yourself. It is amazing how this process can mold and transform both your awareness and the reality which surrounds you.

LIFE *Transition Altars*

Ancient cultures honored the cyclical nature of life with ceremonies celebrating the passage of the seasons or with rituals marking an individual's journey from one stage of his or her life into another. Life Transition Altars are used to mark and to celebrate, or sometimes to mourn, the various passages which are a part of every person's sojourn on this beautiful planet.

Modern life is noticeably lacking this type of ceremony. We celebrate the remnants of ancient rituals in our modern holidays, which roughly correspond to the solstices and equinoxes of the year, but our customary Easters and Christmases have become highly commercialized and estranged from their primary origins.

Life Transition Altars honor the significant events of your journey through life

Similarly, significant events in our lives are often marked only by the briefest of ceremonies. The birth of a child in much of the modern world is the occasion for a baby shower and presents, but these often lack a spiritual dimension and therefore do not fully acknowledge or honor the amazing phenomenon of new life.

Celebrating the seasons of our lives and our earth at the home altar can be an essential way of filling this gap. Creating altars to mark the passing of time and honor the significant events of our lives fulfills an ancient and universal need. The following is a sampling of suggestions for how to create these altars that acknowledge the rites of passage in our lives.

New Relationships Altar

Entering into a new love relationship, getting married, having a baby, starting a new job, enrolling at a different school, moving into a new neighborhood or joining a club are all examples of a passage from one life experience into another. Each change brings new and different types of relationships. An altar that honors the beginning of new relationships can help strengthen them.

When deciding what to place on the New Relationships Altar, think of the qualities you would like to develop in your relationships over time, and find objects that represent those qualities. For example, to create an effective metaphor for your new job, you might create a small circle of pebbles in the center of the altar with each stone representing one of your co-workers, as

well as a stone to symbolize yourself. This could be an effective symbol of how you and your co-workers are in a circle of harmony in friendship and common endeavor. Every time you look at the circle of stones you will be subliminally reminded of your developing relationships.

New Love Altar

Beginnings are important and should be nurtured, and a New Love Altar can be a focal point for celebrating your new love relationship. This type of home shrine helps generate beneficial energy to help sustain the relationship into the future. On this altar place a happy photo of you and your lover as an affirmation of future happiness and contentment. You might also consider placing items that remind you of the nice times that you have shared – the ticket stub from the theater you attended on your first date, dried flower petals from a special bouquet or a colorful leaf you found on a walk together.

This Marriage Altar includes corn for fertility and abundance, toys for playfulness, roses for love, cut crystals for spirituality, and light and candles for joy.

Marriage Altar

The creation of a Marriage Altar can be wonderful and exhilarating. It can be assembled on the day of the wedding and can have symbolic representations of blessings for the future of the couple. For example, a pot or basket can be placed on the altar containing blessings and good wishes, in written form, from each person who attends the wedding. In this way the joyous feelings generated on the wedding day continue to radiate from the wedding basket into the home through the years. In addition, symbols for a strong marriage can be placed on the altar, such as a stone for a well-grounded relationship, a crystal for light and spirituality, corn kernels for fertility and a toy for playfulness during the marriage.

D
S Z
C J
A
R

New Baby Altar

The New Baby Altar can be a sacred area that is always growing and changing with the growth of the child. It can have photos of the baby, blessings from others, a healthy plant dedicated to the health and well-being of the child, a spiritual icon to represent the child's connection to Spirit and a small statue of an angel representing the child's guardian angel. The baby altar can also be the repository of a first lock of hair, childhood teeth and first drawings. When the child becomes older, he or she may want to participate in the evolving creation of this sacred place. If you have more than one child, you might consider one altar or sacred place for each child.

Rite of Passage Altar

Ancient cultures understood the importance of honoring the entrance into adulthood and special ceremonies were often performed. Offerings were made and usually there was a formal ritual of welcoming children into their new status. A Rite of Passage Altar can help bring this past custom into present times. Gather the family together to co-create the altar. Have each family member place an object on the altar that represents the new relationship dynamic that is emerging as the child is entering into more maturity. At the completion of the ceremony, celebrate with a meal.

Seasonal Altar

Traditionally people all over the world have used altars in conjunction with ceremonies to celebrate the seasons and the movement of the celestial bodies. In urban life, however, we have become separated from the greater cycles of nature that are occurring outside our insulated lives. The Seasonal Altar is an excellent way to help reinstate these rhythms of nature into our lives because it honors and acknowledges the cyclical patterns of life, and brings the energy of nature into the home. This type of altar should be renewed with ceremony four times a year – at the solstices and equinoxes.

The objects you place on a Seasonal Altar should be representations of that particular season. For example, in a Spring Altar you might place fresh flowers, a bowl of spring rain and seeds representing new beginnings. This altar is an excellent place to begin the internal process toward initiating new projects into your life.

A Summer Altar might contain symbols of expansion, abundance and prosperity. For example, you might use summer flowers, gold, candles, lush fabrics and anything sparkling and bright. If there is an area of your life that you would like to expand, for example if you would like to gain more

This New Baby Altar includes guardian angels, toys for joy, a photo of the child and an empty space to indicate that all possibilities are open for the child's future.

responsibility at your job, you could use the energy of the Summer Altar to affirm your desire.

Autumn is the time of harvest, so if there is anything in your life that you wish to reap or complete, you could place an object that represents your desires on your Autumn Altar. This type of altar might have a bunch of wheat stalks bundled together, colorful fallen leaves and a photo or drawing of an autumn scene.

The winter is a time for turning within, consolidating your energy and incubating new ideas. To create a Winter Altar you might have a sparse setting with a single photo of a snow-covered mountain or a black or dark-colored altar cloth. If there is an aspect of your life that needs cohesion and consolidation you could use the energy of the Winter Altar to affirm your desire.

A Spring Altar, created at the equinox, containing eggs, flowers and a rabbit, which all symbolize and celebrate new beginnings.

Medicine Wheel Altar

A Medicine Wheel Altar is one that is based on the Native American philosophy of the sacred circle. It is a physical representation of the sacred circle that encompasses life. In its deepest sense, the Medicine Wheel Altar represents all the great cycles of life, including the cycle of birth and death and rebirth, the yearly cycle of the seasons, the four basic elements of life (air, water, fire and earth) and the four directions.

A Medicine Wheel Altar is usually made in the form of a circle with four defined parts. This can be done by placing four objects around the circumference to represent each of the four directions: east, south, west and north. The objects are usually placed on the magnetic compass points. Often a medicine wheel arrangement is created by making a circle of small stones, with four special or larger stones placed around the circle to mark each of the four

Far left: A Medicine Wheel Altar created in a garden with stones and pebbles. Left: A tiny version made with stones and shells.

directions. However, small pine cones, shells, dried flowers or any other natural objects can be used to make the circle. You can also draw a medicine wheel or sew a medicine wheel design into cloth. It is the intent and love that goes into creating an altar, not the prescribed form, that endows it with power.

A Medicine Wheel Altar can be made on a shelf or mantel on a wall. However, it can also be placed on a circular coffee table, on the floor or even outdoors. If you have enough space to make a really large circle for your altar, it can be used as a place that you can sit in for your meditations. Meditating within this sacred circle shrine can be a very moving experience.

Meditating at a Medicine Wheel Altar can connect you to the sacred cycles of your life

Before you create a Medicine Wheel Altar, it is important to understand some of its significance. Gaining the knowledge of what every compass point of the medicine wheel represents will empower your altar. Although there are variants in meaning from one Native American tribe to another, the following are some associations for the cardinal points of the medicine wheel.

East: Symbolically the beginning of the medicine wheel is in the east. Native Americans believe that the east is the home of new beginnings. It symbolizes the spring, the dawning of the day,

The center of the Medicine Wheel Altar represents the Creator and the meeting point between the visible and invisible realms.

and the waxing of the new moon. It contains within it the excitement of new life and new birth. It represents the time when seeds are planted and new sprouts begin pushing up through the darkness of the soil into the light of the sun. The east can represent the element of air and your own mental powers.

South: The southern point of your Medicine Wheel Altar symbolizes the summer, the midday sun and the full moon. Crops are high. Days are long and full of midsummer warmth. It is a time of fullness and expansion. The south is associated with a time of rapid growth and the time of childhood. The south may represent water and the emotional part of yourself.

West: The western point of your altar is associated with the autumn, the setting sun and the waning moon. Abundant crops are harvested and stored. In the human cycle, west is associated with the young adult years, as these are the years of change, entering maturity, discovery, transformation and experimentation. The west can represent fire and the spiritual side of Self.

North: The northern point represents the realm of winter, the darkest, longest nights and the dark phase of the moon. It also symbolizes completion and consolidation. In the human cycle the north is associated with the achievement of maturity, the accomplishments of the middle years of life and the transition to old age. It is a time of honor for the elders, the grandmothers and grandfathers, the wise ones. The north embodies the magic of the cycle of death and rebirth as well as representing the earth and the physical aspect of Self.

Center of the Wheel: Together, the four cardinal points of the Medicine Wheel Altar represent all the inner and outer cycles of life. However, the most sacred part of this altar is the center because it symbolizes the Creator and the meeting point between the visible and invisible realms. Early mystics of many traditions understood the sanctity of the center of the sacred circle. They used it as a focal point to commune with the Divine. When you use your Medicine Wheel Altar for reflection and contemplation, you are entering into a respected tradition that honors all aspects of your life as well as the source of all life.

THE Completion Altar

Endings are as important as beginnings, and an altar is an excellent place to honor the completion of a cycle in life. Completing the cycle makes it easier to begin a new one.

The Death of a Loved One

Our culture is bereft of ceremonies that pay homage to the cycle of death and that encourage healing through the grieving process. The short duration of a funeral does not encompass the long period of grieving which was incorporated into the death ceremonies of earlier times in various cultures. Many people today are not affiliated with religious traditions that fully recognize the loss created by death, and so frequently they don't have appropriate means to experience and release their sadness.

An altar offers a holistic way to honor and say good-bye to someone who has passed on. This process helps heal the sorrow caused by their departure. If you have experienced the loss of someone close to you or even a beloved pet, you might put a photo of the loved one in a special place in your home. Next to the photo you could place mementos of the relationship, such as letters, special gifts received from the loved one and objects that represent special shared

memories. You might decide to light a candle periodically to give thanks for all that you gained from the relationship and to wish the individual a good journey into the hereafter. This kind of altar can be used for a short period following a death. Or it can be used over a twelve-month cycle, which is a traditional amount of time set aside for grieving and healing in many cultures.

Completion of a Relationship

As we grow and change there are times when we may begin to travel on a different path from someone with whom we once felt very close. This is a natural phenomenon, although it is often accompanied by much pain. The trauma and difficulty often caused by such departures can be lessened by ceremonially honoring the end of the relationship. A Completion Altar can assist this process. For example, following a divorce, a Completion Altar might have separate photos of each individual on opposite sides of the altar divided by a clear boundary line, signifying that the marriage bond is severed so that each person can go on with their own life.

Children Growing Up and Leaving Home

An altar is an excellent place to honor the completion of one phase of raising children as they prepare to leave home. This type of altar might have a high school graduation photo and something signifying the child's growing independence. An example of this would be a feather, chosen to represent the child taking flight and leaving the nest to make a place of their own in the world. Any object that symbolizes the end of one phase and the beginning of another for you and for your child would be appropriate.

Completion of a Job or Project, or Graduation

It is often difficult to enter a new job or embark on a new project if you haven't emotionally let go of the old one. A Completion Altar can help you symbolically to let go of your attachment to an old career, school or employment with which you strongly identified. This in turn helps you to focus your energy in a new direction. For example, if you are ready to leave your career as a gardener and move toward a career as a massage therapist, then you might make a bundle of a small pile of seeds, some miniature garden tools and soil and wrap this bundle with cording to represent the fact that your gardening days are complete. This could be placed at the back of the altar. A small beautiful bottle of scented massage oil could be placed in the center of the altar to represent your new career as a massage therapist.

A simple Memorial Altar for a favorite grandfather.

RSA
7319
Seattle, Washington
98115
USA
Ref. No. 90
Huh?

SPECIAL *Occasion Altars*

Holiday Altar

In some cultures special holidays are honored with a Holiday Altar. For example, in Japan once a year for the Bon Festival, offerings of herbs, flowers and food are placed on the family shrine to honor the ancestors. During the Christmas holidays, in some cultures, a special Christmas Altar is created that has a nativity scene with small wooden or plaster figurines of Joseph, Mary and the baby Jesus as well as an assortment of animals, shepherds and Wise Men.

Creating a Holiday Altar not only brings a feeling of celebration into your home, but in a more profound sense it pays homage to the deeper meaning underlying the holidays. You can either follow traditional motifs or use your creativity. For example, you might consider making a May Day (Beltane) Holiday Altar by placing fresh spring flowers, boughs of greenery, ribbons, objects made of wood and flower garlands to honor the fertility of the coming season. A New Year's Eve or Winter Solstice Altar could have offerings and candles and an urn to be a symbolic repository for your dreams for the coming year, as well as a place to release old memories and experiences from the year past. As you create a Holiday

This Holiday Altar honors the rebirth of the sun at the winter solstice.

Previous pages: A Vacation Altar filled with mementos of a joyous summer vacation beside the sea.

Altar, with every step of the process you are acknowledging the sacred dimension underlying each traditional holiday.

Anniversary Altar

An Anniversary Altar can be used for events such as wedding anniversaries or to honor an annual commemoration of an important family event. For example, one family honors the day that their great-grandfather single-handedly saved a town from a flood by running 15 miles in the dark to alert everyone. This remarkable event is marked every year by placing a candle on the altar in front of his picture, next to a glass of wine which symbolically represents a toast to his heroic effort.

Vacation Altar

A unique way to use your altar space is to create a Vacation Altar. For example, imagine that you had a wonderful holiday at the seashore. Everything was perfect. The sky was blue. The air was clear. Each day flowed smoothly into the next, bringing fresh adventures and new friends. To maintain some of the energy and joy that you experienced on your vacation, you could place on your altar the beautiful piece of driftwood that you found at dawn early one morning. You might also include the pieces of turquoise and blue frosted beach glass that you gathered from the shore's edge. Objects that remind you of your holiday can help keep the joy and excitement that you felt during those special days alive throughout the rest of the year.

After a trip to Venice, this Vacation Altar was created with souvenirs and reminders of the holiday.

Birthday Altar

A Birthday Altar can be renewed every year on your birthday. On this altar you can put items that represent your hopes and desires for the coming year. For example, if you desire more peace for the coming twelve months, take a moment to discover what might symbolize peace to you. Perhaps a deep purple amethyst crystal, a small beautiful glass bowl filled with spring water and a statue of a meditating Buddha all resting easily on a beautiful cobalt blue altar cloth would together give you a feeling of serenity. Every time you look at this altar, it will radiate the peaceful feeling and will help you move toward greater peace for your coming year.

A Birthday Altar filled with symbols that represent hopes for the coming year: a butterfly for joy, dolls for creativity and photos for love.

THE *Protection Altar*

Altars can be used to help generate a protective energy around your home. To create a Protection Altar, place objects on it that give you a feeling of safety and protection. These may be very personal and individual. For one person a statue of the Archangel Michael with his sword held high will feel protective, while for another a figure of an angel or a framed copy of the Lord's Prayer may feel protective. For someone else, the six-pointed Star of Solomon or a picture of a saint might make them feel safe. For your altar to generate a true protective energy, you must use ceremony and ritual when creating it. In addition, you need to renew your altar periodically through energizing it, either by prayer or mantras or meditation. (See pages 135–140.)

An angel on a Protection Altar helps generate a protective energy around your home.

MEMORIAL AND *Ancestral Altars*

In many cultures a shrine, altar or designated portion of the home is reserved for the ancestors and deceased family members where daily offerings of food, incense and flowers are placed. Mementos or physical representations of the departed ancestors are placed on the family altar and homage is paid to them on a regular basis. Many people believe that, by doing this, they receive the help of their ancestors during their life. Having healthy children, abundant wealth and personal safety are all believed to be dependent on making proper and timely gifts to one's forebears. This type of altar is called an Ancestral Altar.

Ancestors Today

If you decide to create an Ancestral Altar it doesn't necessarily mean that you are worshipping your ancestors; it is more like a reminder of the special place of honor that they hold within your life. One way of looking at our ancestors and deceased family members is to see them as a long, continuous line of people who have faced and overcome the same struggles that we confront in our lives.

The successes and failures of those who came before us helped to shape the reality of our own lives, just as our actions will affect the generations who follow us. Including remembrances of ancestors and family members in a special place in your home is a valuable way of honoring their continuing presence and contribution to your life. By honoring our ancestors and deceased relatives, we are reminded that life doesn't end when we die. By using ceremony and ritual in conjunction with an Ancestral Altar, we can make it a visible symbol of an invisible reality that marks our part of a unified lineage of humankind.

Honoring past and future generations at an altar helps to remind us that life is eternal

The Ancestral Altar is especially valuable if there has been strife, turmoil or even dysfunctional behavior which has passed down through the generations. It can help make whole that which has been damaged. Honoring your ancestors can result in the healing of troubled relationships. If you have conflicting feelings about family members, these problems can be addressed and resolved by finding a way to include them in your home altar. Childhood photographs of persons you may now have some difficulty with can allow you to connect with them at a time when they were lovable.

Feathers, a medicine bag, a rattle and photographs of my grandmother are key elements of my Ancestral Altar.

If you feel estranged from the culture you grew up in, you might want to find some small part of it that did feel good to you and represent that on your Ancestral Altar. This can sow a small seed of emotional resolution which can grow into the healing of old issues as you continue to meditate and pray in the presence of these images. Coming to terms with our backgrounds is an important part of personal synthesis and healing. The home altar can be a vital catalyst in that process.

The Memorial Altar

A Memorial Altar is similar to an Ancestral Altar but is not necessarily dedicated to your forebears. It can serve as a memorial to friends who have passed on, or it can be used as a remembrance of someone who was important to you. For example, when Princess Diana died, many people placed a candle in front of her photo as a way to honor her memory.

A Memorial Altar can also honor family members that are yet to be born – our descendants. It can hold objects that symbolize qualities that you wish to pass on to your descendants. A Memorial Altar can be a loving reminder of the emotional and physical legacies that we are passing down to our children, their children and their children's children.

Creating a Memorial or Ancestral Altar

This type of altar can be as simple as a collection of photos. Or it can be more elaborate, such as a built-in alcove with special lighting. You can have an area dedicated to your ancestors on a general home altar or you can have a special altar specifically dedicated to those you desire to remember. In addition to favorite photos of your forebears or friends, you can also have objects on the altar that are symbolic of qualities that you perceive in those you wish to memorialize. For example, you might include a beautiful shell that you picked up on a visit to your grandmother's seaside cottage. The shell will always remind you of your grandmother's nurturing love. This kind of altar can also be a gathering place for associations and memories and symbols of the past, so that they may be synthesized into your present life.

Cultural and Family Traditions

On an Ancestral Altar you might choose to emphasize certain traditions which have been handed down in your family or your culture. Including traditional objects or performing traditional rituals from your family or cultural heritage can be a way of keeping those traditions alive for future generations.

A Jewish family's Memorial Altar honoring religious traditions and family members who have passed on.

שבת
שלום
כוס אליהו
Elijah Cup

Many people come from more than one cultural heritage. In deciding which tradition to honor on your altar, let your feelings be your guide. One part of your cultural endowment might have meaning for one part of your life, while another side better meets your needs in another area or at another time in your life. There is no one right way to approach this issue. All of the different elements of our background have value and can enrich our lives, and they can contribute to the richness and significance of the home altar.

Day of the Dead

In Spanish-speaking countries, the use of the Memorial Altar is especially prevalent during the Day of the Dead, which is one of the most important religious holy days of the year. To the people of Mexico, where it is an honor and a duty to commemorate family members and friends that have died, this tradition can be traced back to the Aztec religion. The Aztecs believed that death was not an ending but the beginning of a new and eternal existence, and thus they respected the cycle of life by honoring the dead. The current Day of the Dead has evolved to become a mixture of pre-Columbian beliefs and the Roman Catholic religion. It is celebrated on November 1st, which is also All Saint's Day.

On the Day of the Dead, home altars are decorated with candles, sugar cane stalks and arches made out of marigolds. Flower petal carpets lead to the altar, on which special food is placed. Photographs of the departed are put on the home altar, usually close to pictures of religious beings such as Jesus or saints or angels to honor and remember those who have passed away.

There are occasions when it is difficult to trace one's roots fully. For instance, if your ancestors were immigrants who traveled to the United States from Ireland, and you don't know much else about them, then you might imagine the fortitude and inner strength that they must have possessed to strike out for a new land. To honor their sacrifices and courage, you might place on your Ancestral Altar the feather of a migrating bird that travels great distances.

You can also include objects on your home altar that have been in your family for a long time, such as an old clay cup that has been passed down through the generations. Alternatively, you can use something that symbolizes your predecessors to you, such as a piece of driftwood if your people lived near the sea.

Your Ancestral Altar can contribute to honoring the past, celebrating the present and envisioning the future. It can create a powerful metaphor for honoring and uniting with your personal past. Including a memorial to departed family members in your sacred space is a way of keeping the trust that our predecessors placed in us, which we will in turn pass on to our children and others whom we love. It is an ancient tradition that deserves reviving.

A Day of the Dead Altar commemorating family members and friends who have passed on.

THE Inner Child Altar

An Inner Child Altar can be a wondrous experience to create, and it can also help begin to heal childhood wounds. Many people have had a less-than-perfect childhood. The pain from the past often lurks in the heart, sometimes negatively affecting relationships and important life experiences. An Inner Child Altar can create a powerful metaphor for beginning to heal the wounded child that still hungers for love, acceptance and happiness.

To create an Inner Child Altar, take some time to go into a relaxed state and imagine yourself as a child laughing and feeling delighted with life. Notice what and who are around you. When you come out of your contemplation, find objects for your altar that symbolize the wonderful experiences you had in the meditation. For example, on an Inner Child Altar you might put a container of bubble soap for blowing bubbles, a wind-up yellow duck, a well-loved doll, and a childlike drawing that you have created of yourself looking happy. Put anything that is representative of simpler and more innocent times. This kind of altar can bring a spirit of joy, spontaneity and fun into a home and can help you begin to heal a difficult childhood.

An Inner Child Altar filled with toys, bright colors and flowers to call forth joy and fun.

THE *Garden Altar*

A garden can be a place to take refuge from the activity of day-to-day living. It can be a place that allows you to collect your thoughts and refocus your life. An altar in a garden can form a synthesis and focal point for the nurturing energy of the garden. Additionally, using an outdoor shrine can be a sacred and even holy act, for it can deeply and profoundly help to reconnect you back to your roots, which dwell in the land, the rocks, the trees, the sky and the clouds. It can carry you back to the earliest of times when our ancestors used outdoor altars to invoke and heed the mystical cycles of nature.

A Garden Altar can incorporate the plants and landscape in its creation, but ideally the view should be defined by some frame, such as a tree trunk, a gazebo or an alcove. Always at the core of a Garden Altar is a central point to bring sacred energy into the garden. It is valuable to have a place from which you can view your garden altar, such as a carefully placed bench. The best Garden Altars offer a feeling of intimacy, protection and privacy.

Garden Altar for Contemplation

A Contemplative Garden Altar contributes to a tranquil state of peace and reflection. In the beauty of a garden, the altar becomes the focal point for the union between people and nature. Concentrating on the altar, there often comes a point when the viewer transcends the form of the garden and the altar and enters into a deep state of peace and awareness. After this experience there is often a sense of renewal and joy that permeates all other aspects of life. This kind of shrine or altar might include a statue of Buddha or St. Francis surrounded by plants in the soothing colors of soft blues, greens and white. In addition you might want to plant some lavender nearby, as its scent has a relaxing effect.

The properties of water are universally soothing – a mountain stream cascading and tumbling, a still mountain pool, the sound and smell of rain during a summer storm – so your Contemplation Altar might be a good place to install a fountain or pond. Even a small clay pot, to catch rain, on your altar can be a reminder of the spiritually rejuvenating yet relaxing element of water.

Creating a sacred shrine in the garden connects us to our roots and provides a focal point for peaceful contemplation

Another type of Contemplative Altar is the Zen garden. The Zen garden, which has its roots in Shintoism, is a large carefully constructed area of groomed gravel and strategically placed rocks. They have a highly significant symbolism and they are thought to express the deepest mysteries of the universe. Just sitting still and viewing the simplicity and grace of a Zen garden is said to allow one to enter into deep states of inner peace. You can make a similar type of shrine by artistically placing large rocks in raked and patterned gravel. Traditionally, Zen gardens are composed of an uneven number of rocks, usually in threes, which represent Heaven, Earth and Humans.

Garden Altar for Rapture

A Garden Altar for Rapture is exhilarating. It expands all the senses with expressive movement and vitality. For this type of garden altar, you might consider a fountain with water splashing in a carefree manner, or a bright glass garden ball, found in nurseries and garden stores, surrounded by a riot of flower colors and textures, or wind chimes hung from a tree branch to gently ring in the breeze. Contrasting qualities, such as a roughly hewn rock surrounded by soft ferns, heighten the senses and create an abundant environment for your perceptions. A statue of a dancing fairy or a joyous flute-playing Pan might make an excellent focus. This kind of altar will bring life force and energy into your garden and into your life.

Mystical Garden Altar

This type of altar can act as a mystical door into other realms. It should have a sense of seclusion and mystery. A Mystical Garden Altar gradually moves the viewer from one state of mind to another. For this kind of altar you might place natural quartz crystals in the earth so their facets can catch the sun, or place a statue of Merlin or a celestial angel slightly hidden among dark green foliage, or hang cut crystals from branches to generate rainbow lights, or create a simple waterfall or still pool. Consider planting flowers that range in color from lavender to deep purple and violet, with plants of silver foliage as a backdrop. This altar can be a place where you can still your thoughts and enter into inner realms of the wondrous and mysterious.

You can also make a Mystical Garden Altar out of stones. The very earliest altars were either a large stone or a pile of stones indicating a sacred place, often thought to mark an intersection between the visible and invisible realms, and travelers and pilgrims would leave offerings at these cairns. Today, creating a stone altar in your garden can activate ancestral memories of the power of these shrines of the past. Your altar can be a mystical gateway to other realms that can align you with the deep mysteries of the land.

The Zen garden creates an outdoor shrine of repose and tranquility.

Divine Feminine Garden Altar

Creating a sacred place in a garden that honors the Divine Feminine force can bring a sacred and holy energy to the surrounding area. A statue of an African goddess, the Virgin Mary or Venus can be a focal point in your garden altar to call forth the receptive feminine energies of Mother Earth and to honor the creative forces in the universe. Planting fragrant flowers is a way to enhance the beauty of this area.

Another type of Divine Feminine Altar honors the Earth Goddess. To create this kind of altar, you have to fashion it out of the earth itself. In native and ancient cultures throughout the world, outdoor altars were constructed with mounds of earth. Although these earthen altars are thought to have been used in a number of ways, one of the most powerful uses was as a symbol of the Earth Goddess.

This type of altar can be made in many ways, shapes and sizes. However, the most powerful earthen altars are those that are created in a sacred way, in which you reach your hands into the soil feeling its texture, smelling its rich aroma and connecting with the deep and primal rhythms of the land. You can either leave the mound bare or you can plant it with seeds – either way, this type of altar contains the essence of a primordial female wisdom.

Wild Garden Altar

A Wild Garden Altar can have a number of functions. It can help bring out your wild side, and it can be a place to invite wildlife, fairies and elementals into your garden. A Wild Garden Altar should not be too carefully cultivated and groomed because it needs to have a life of its own. Encourage the growth of plants that attract birds and butterflies. Put up birdhouses and bird feeders. Sprinkle corn for the squirrels. Sprinkle handfuls of wildflower seeds on the earth. Do anything that encourages wildlife and nature and life force. For a focal point, you might put a statue of an elf, dwarf or fairy, or a large natural stone or a statue of a wild animal such as a bear or deer, in the center of the area.

Trees or bushes can also be used as focal points in Wild Garden Altars. In past generations trees were used as altars because they were seen as the connection between the heavens and the earth. It was also thought that every tree contained a guardian spirit which empowered the surrounding environment. To use your tree or bush for your altar you can tie prayer flags, wind chimes, ornaments or feathers on the branches, or you can allow the innate beauty and strength of the plant to speak for itself. Sitting before a Wild Garden Altar encourages creativity and deepens your connection to nature and all things natural.

A Kwan Yin statue in a garden creates a focal point that calls forth the Divine Feminine energy into the garden.

ALTARS *Away from Home*

Your altars need not be restricted to your home and yard – you can create altars wherever you are. Whether a small portable altar for travel, a workplace altar or a spontaneously created altar, every personal shrine carries a reminder of the larger spiritual principles at play in our life.

Workplace Altar

The value of an altar in your office or workplace is that it creates a positive energy field around you. Many people work in environments that are isolated from fresh air and natural sunlight, and in these surroundings it is essential to the well-being of your soul to have a place that feels sacred. A Workplace Altar can instill a sense of the hallowed amid the usually harried work surroundings.

Many office and work environments, however, are not receptive to altars, so this is a time when the subliminal altar can be helpful. By choosing one place on your desk or in your workplace and clustering photographs of loved ones, a small framed significant quote, a vase of fresh flowers, a healthy plant or even a beautiful piece of ripe fruit, you have made a lovely sacred place that will radiate a special energy that will engulf you, your desk and the surrounding area. Perhaps no one will be consciously aware of your altar, but they will perceive the harmonious energy around you and your desk.

Spontaneous Altar

Sometimes altars which are created spontaneously bring a sense of cosmic order and harmony to their surroundings. Once when I was on holiday with some friends at the seashore, I found a wonderful large stone that had been molded by the sea. I carefully placed it in the sand and drew a circle around it. A friend approached with an armful of shells she had collected and placed them in a unique design in front of the stone. Another friend dragged some driftwood up the shore to place at the back of the stone. All of this occurred naturally and spontaneously. There was a point when simultaneously we all knew it was complete. Sitting together in silence before our altar as the sun slowly sank beneath the sea was a remarkable experience. It seemed as if the energy of the sun, sky and sea was magnified through our Spontaneous Altar deep into the heart of each of us.

A figurine of White Tara, the maternal Tibetan goddess, flowers and crystals form an altar on a desk.

THE *creation*

THE *Creation*

The creation of an altar is a sacred act. To empty your mind and open your heart to an energy greater than yourself, while you assemble your special objects, is an act of power and grace. For a few timeless moments you enter into a dimension beyond ordinary reality where light, sound and energy merge into an exquisite state of being. During this time, as you transcend your own normal perception, your altar becomes infused with a remarkable life-force energy that will continue to emanate from it forever.

Creating your home altar is a remarkably fulfilling act for several reasons. Not only does the act of assembling the altar objects imbue a spiritual energy into the home environment, but the decision-making process that occurs beforehand is also empowering. Taking the time to choose carefully what to place on your altar provides a unique opportunity to examine your inner values and discover what really matters to you. Each object on your altar represents a different quality or an aspect of your life, and the thoughtful selection of each item begins to allow you to gain clarity about what is truly important for you.

From the moment that you decide to construct an altar until its completion, the process of creating an altar is holy. Although there are various kinds of and different uses for your personal shrines, there are four steps which are common to their creation: Preparation, Purification, Invocation and Preservation. Taking time and care with each step deepens the value that you will gain over the years from your altar.

Preparation

The first step in preparing to make an altar is to become clear about its purpose. This step forms a foundation for each of the steps that are to follow. Once you are certain about why you are making an altar, you will need to make some decisions, such as where you will locate it in your home, how big it will be and what objects you will place on it.

Intention

The most important step in the creation of an altar is establishing your intention for it. What is its main purpose? Subsequent decisions about layout and structure will be affected and even determined by your reason for creating it. Your intention for your altar is the foundation upon which the entire outcome of your altar rests, so it is vital to take the time necessary to become clear about this initial stage. For example, if the focus of your altar is to increase peace in your life, and yet on your altar there is an object that makes you feel sad, then this element will not contribute to your objective of peace. However, if your purpose is to clear away unresolved grief from your past, then this same altar object will be helpful for bringing old issues to the surface where they can be consciously processed and released.

In clarifying your overall goals, it can be very helpful to imagine yourself sitting in front of your completed altar. What do you hope to accomplish by having it in your home? What parts of your life will it represent? Do you primarily want a quiet place where you can center your thoughts and achieve deep inner stillness, or do you want your altar to be an alcove for photos of family members that provides a sense of connection to your extended family? Perhaps there are some qualities that you desire. Do you want more love in your life? The box below will help you clarify the purpose of your altar. Even if the options don't apply to you exactly, they will point you in the right direction.

Creating an altar is an act of power and grace

It is vital that you take the time to discover the underlying purpose for your altar. It is also important to ask yourself why you want to have an altar. The clearer you are about your overall objectives, the more focused and dynamic the energy fields surrounding you altar will become.

An altar can help you to

- Commune with the Divine
- Heal family relationships
- Open your life to love
- Bring the spirit of nature into your home
- Create vibrant health
- Honor your transitions in life
- Create wealth and abundance
- Open up creative channels
- Honor your ancestors and family connections
- Celebrate yourself
- Commemorate achievements/losses in your life
- Celebrate cultural, ethnic and/or religious traditions
- Honor the yearly cycle and the cycles within yourself
- Remember loved ones that have passed on
- Integrate the various aspects of yourself

A helpful tool for clarifying your goals is to envision the specific, long-term results you hope to achieve from your altar. For example, if your intention for your altar is for healing, a specific result you desire might be that everyone in your home be healthy and strong. Another person who also had an intention for a healing altar might hope to be more effective in their professional practice of homeopathy. Someone else might focus specifically on healing a particular debilitating disease. Gaining awareness about the results that you want to achieve can help you become clear about the reason for your altar.

It is not necessary to have only one purpose for your altar. Altars can fulfill many different kinds of functions in your life, and the most vibrant altars often change over time as needs and interests change. Multi-purpose altars are probably much more common than single-purpose ones because they can be useful for synthesizing many levels of life's complexities. Multi-purpose altars can be a composite for the rich diversity of life and can help you to resolve more complicated issues over time. Single-purpose altars, however, can be especially powerful because they focus all of your energy on one area of your life.

Not all altars are used for meditation purposes; however, if you do use your altar as a focal point for contemplative practices, know that there is a direct connection between the intention for your altar and the results produced by your practices. An altar can magnify and project the energy of your meditations, so the more care that you take in the creation of it, the greater will be the effects which follow.

Altar Placement in the Home

Once you are clear about your intention, you are ready to decide where you will place an altar in your home. Every area of a home or building has a different energy, and each room will influence the feeling of your altar in a specific way. Taking the time to decide where you will place your altar can affect the overall results you will attain from using your personal shrine.

"Heart of the Home"

One excellent place to situate an altar is in the heart of the home. I like to think that every home has a heart. It is the area in any home that feels the most special, the most vital to the energy of the place. In some homes, this heart might correspond with the physically central part of the house, but this is not always the case.

I once knew a family who lived in a beautiful farmhouse with a huge kitchen. In this kitchen there was a lovely old oak table. Family members would often gather around this table to talk about the events of their day while meals were being prepared and consumed. If you had asked any of them where the heart of their home was, I know that they would have said the kitchen, even though it was at the back of the main floor. For them this room was a natural place to put a warm, earthy altar celebrating family communion and love, because it was truly the heart of their home.

In some homes, no room seems to dominate or have more significance than any of the others. If this is the case with you, then you might choose to locate your altar in the physically central portion of your home. This too can represent its heart.

The Four Directions of the Compass

Another way to choose the best location for your altar is to establish your personal shrine according to direction: east, south, west and north. Most ancient mystical traditions honored the four directions and oriented the altar placement accordingly. It was believed that each direction had a different energy. This ancient custom still persists. In some religions, such as the Catholic and Episcopalian, an altar is almost always positioned on the easternmost wall so that the congregation and the priest are facing toward the east – since it is thought that the Resurrection occurred there. Similarly, in many native cultures, ceremonies are conducted facing east because that is the direction of the rising sun – the place where the new day dawns.

Generally the east is considered to be the place of new beginnings because of its association with the sunrise, and it is usually a good area of your home or of a room to create an altar. However, every direction has its strength and beauty. The south is the area of expansion and growth because it is associated with the noon sun. The west is the place for transformation and change and is the place of the setting sun. The north is the realm of the deepest inner dimensions because it is the home of the darkest night. (In the Southern Hemisphere the meanings for the north and the south are reversed.) Placing your altar in a particular direction will magnify the qualities of that direction into your life. Using the cardinal compass points to orient your altar allows you to enter into a time-honored tradition and also connects your inner sacred space with natural forces of the outer world. (For more information about the symbolism of the four directions, see the section on the Medicine Wheel Altar on pages 58–61.)

Choosing the Room for Your Altar

Each room in your home has a different feeling and energy, and your altar will be influenced by the room within which it is placed. For example, the bedroom would be good place for an altar dedicated to romantic love. A young newlywed wanted to deepen the relationship with her husband, so on the bedroom dresser she created an altar. In the center of the altar she placed a lovely statue of a man and woman embracing each other. Next to the couple she placed a small velvet heart-shaped pillow that was filled with fragrant herbs. In addition, she placed a happy photo of herself and her husband taken during their vacation by the sea. This Love Altar was the first thing that she and her husband saw every morning when they awoke, thus creating a wonderful and loving template for the day.

It's helpful to have at least one altar that is visible from your bed. Not only is it the last thing that you see before you go to sleep and the first you see when you awake, but its energy is a positive influence during your night hours. A bedroom altar can influence your dream states, so it is also a good location for a shrine dedicated to dreams.

The living room is a good place to position an altar to honor friends and family. Your dining room or kitchen is a deserving place for an Abundance Altar because food and nourishment are traditionally associated with prosperity. The area around the hearth or fireplace is excellent for any altar because, in past times, the hearth was considered the heart of the home, no matter where it was placed. In ancient times gods and goddesses were paid homage around the hearth and the burning fire represented the spiritual flame in all beings.

The entrance to your home can be an auspicious place for a Blessing Altar to bring good fortune into your life. In fact, a home threshold is a good location for sacred objects because it symbolizes the gateway between the inner and outer universes. The entrance to a home "sets" the energy for the entire house, because it is the first thing that is viewed when entering, so it lends itself to all types of altars.

One consideration regarding altar placement is how public you want your shrine to be. Some people might feel that their altar is a private and personal concern and may not want it to be seen by visitors. If this is the case with you, choose a room where you can maintain your privacy.

Altar Placement Using the "Bagua"

You can also use feng shui, the ancient Chinese art of placement, to help you decide where to place your home altar. (See my book *Sacred Space* for more information.) Just as we have an energy grid overlying our physical body called the meridian system (which is utilized in acupuncture), so each home is overlapped by an energy grid system called the bagua, according to Chinese philosophy. This grid system over your home influences the energy in each area of the house. Just as reflexology provides us with a map to show which areas of the foot are connected to which areas of the body, each area of your home has a particular quality assigned to it. By placing an altar in a particular area in the home, you deepen its influence and potency. In other words, the essential energy of the bagua amplifies the power of the altar.

An easy way to discover the bagua areas of your home is to draw an aerial picture of your home (this is similar to an architectural-type drawing) and then apply the bagua grid system (shown on page 93) on top of it. If you have more than one floor, the bagua grid (or map) extends all the way up (or down) all the floors. For example, the corner of the home that represents relationships will be the same on every floor. In addition, there isn't a sharp line of demarcation

A Blessing Altar positioned at the front door brings good fortune into the home.

A Home Altar laid out according to the principles of the bagua map.

between one bagua area and another; rather the bagua grid shows the general areas of the home that represent various aspects of your life. The bagua map can also be overlaid on every room in your home by aligning the map with the main entrance to the room. (In other words, your home's entrance will either be in the Inner Knowledge area, the Career area or the Helpful People area.)

In feng shui, each of the nine squares of the bagua relates to some area of your life. For instance, one area of your home relates to Relationships and Marriage. (See the bagua map following.) Using the principles of this ancient system, if you decide to create an altar to bring more love into your life, a good place for it would be in the Relationships area of either your home

Bagua map for your house

Wealth, Blessings & Abundance	Fame, Self-expression & Reputation	Relationships & Marriage
Family, Ancestors & Heritage	Health	Projects & Children
Inner Knowledge & Self-realization	Career & Path in Life	Helpful People & Angels

Align front door to your home along this line

Above is a bagua map that you can copy and lay over a diagram of your home to see what area of your home aligns with which particular qualities.

or a room within your home. Other appropriate altar choices for the Relationships area of your home could be an altar dedicated to resolving relationship problems, or an altar celebrating the love between you and your partner. If you want to create more abundance and feelings of luxury in your life, a good place for your altar would be the bagua area of your home which is associated with Wealth, Blessings and Abundance. This area would also be suitable for an altar dedicated to gratitude for all of the abundance you already have.

An altar whose primary purpose is for personal synthesis could be effectively placed in the section of your home related to Inner Knowledge and Self-realization. This is also an excellent location for meditation altars and altars devoted to asking for wisdom and communication with the Divine. Another ideal location for an altar dedicated to spirituality would be in the Angels and Helpful People area of your home.

If you want to increase your success in the world, you might place an altar in the Reputation and Fame area. However, if you wish to enhance your career or find your true life calling, then you might consider constructing your altar in the Career area of your home.

Altars honoring one's ancestors or celebrating family connections would be well placed in the bagua area devoted to Ancestors, Family and Heritage. A Fertility Altar might be positioned in the area related to Creativity and Children. Since this area of your home is also associated with new projects, you could also place an altar there to help you birth a new idea or get started on the work you have always dreamed of doing. The center of your home is associated with Health and Life Force Energy, so a Healing Altar would be excellent in the middle of your home.

Example of a bagua map for a bedroom

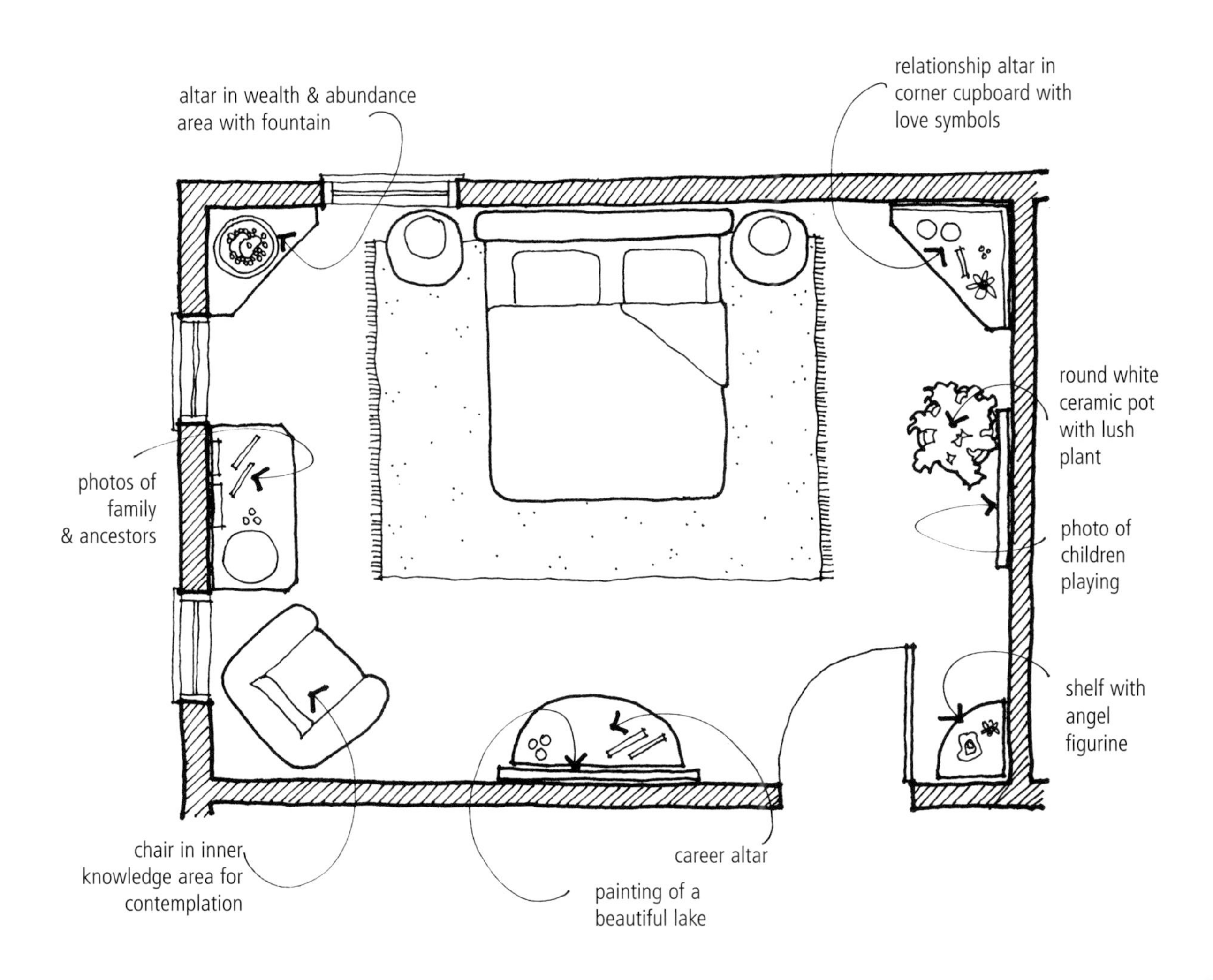

Missing Areas

	Fame, Self-expression & Reputation	Relationships & Marriage
Family, Ancestors Heritage	Health	Projects & Children
Inner Knowledge & Self-realization	Career & Path in Life	Helpful People & Angels

Align front door to your home along this line

Most homes aren't perfect squares but are usually rectangular in shape. If this is the case for your home, then stretch the bagua chart either vertically or horizontally to overlap your home.

If your home is not in a perfect square or rectangle, it is considered to have a "missing part." (See bagua map above.) A traditional Chinese person would never build a house with a missing area, but western architects take no account of this in their designs. In feng shui, it is felt that a missing part can affect your life. For example, someone missing the Wealth area of their home may have financial difficulties. In feng shui, mirrors are one solution to compensate for areas of the home that are missing because they create an illusion of depth so the wall seems to extend into the missing area. To install an altar in an area of your home that is missing an aspect of the bagua map, position your altar close to the missing area and place a mirror behind it. This gives the feeling of depth into the area that is missing so it seems to extend the room. (See drawing below.)

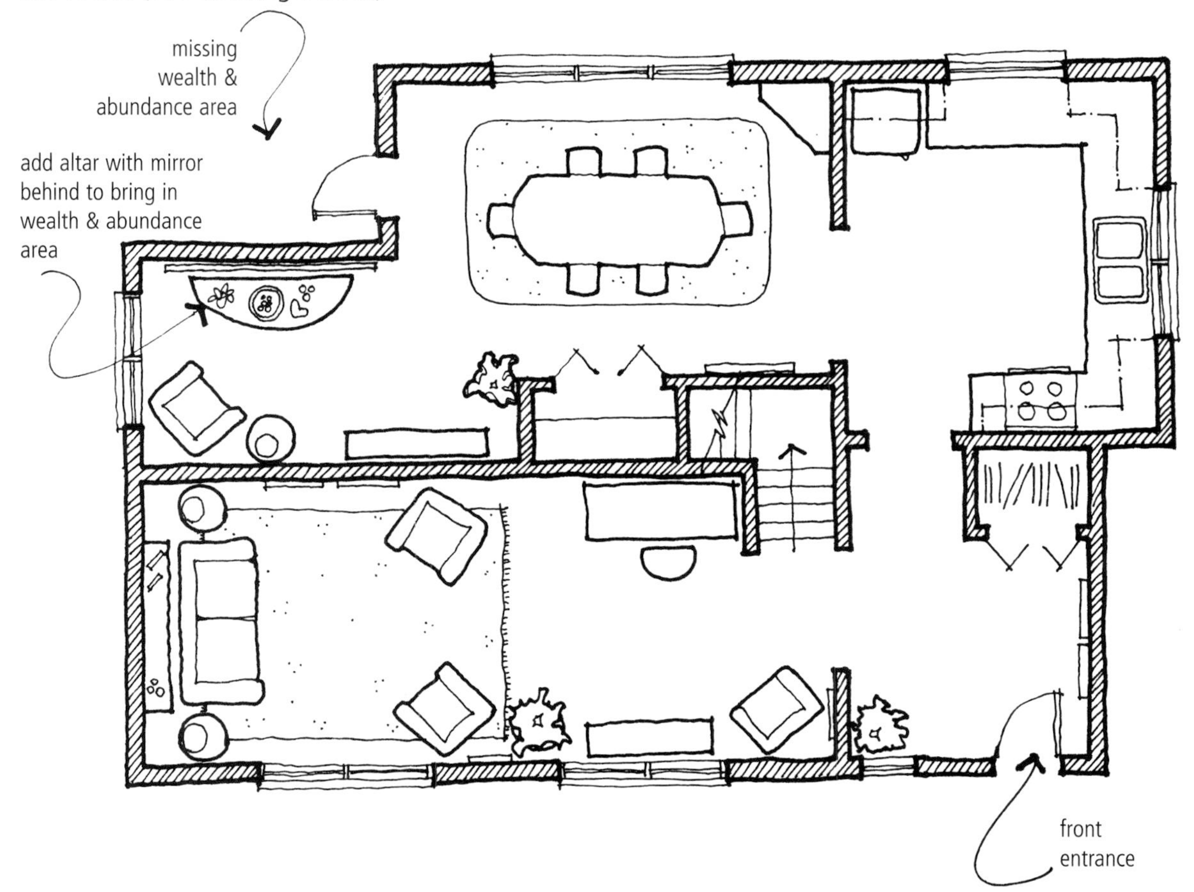

ALTAR *Size and Structure*

When deciding where to place your altar, you may take into account the amount of space you have, convenience, the four directions, feng shui and where you spend most of your time, but ultimately the perfect place is the one you choose through your intuition – the place that just "feels right."

After you have decided where to place your altar, you will need to think about what kind of structure you want for it. The structure is important because it creates the context for your altar. Just as a frame can have a dramatic effect on the way a painting is perceived, so the form and structure of your altar influence its overall feeling. In a deep sense, the form and shape create the energy foundation of your altar, so it is essential to think carefully when making construction decisions about your shrine.

The creation of an altar is a holy act; each step is infused with care

Choosing what kind of altar feels right to you is a significant part of the process. There is no one correct way to construct your altar, and your decisions or your choices will be influenced by your lifestyle and individual needs. No space is too small to make an effective and lovely altar, so don't feel that you have to move to more spacious living quarters before you create one. Size is not important. What matters is combining your clear intention with your very best efforts to create an area that is representative of what is in your heart. I have seen powerful and beautiful altars made on tiny shelves and very small tabletops.

Consider your overall needs and the activities that you do in your home, and then decide how and where the altar could best fit – given these parameters. For instance, if you have small children, you will need to position your altar in a safe place where they cannot pull heavy objects down on their heads. If you live alone in a comparatively large space, then your altar placement considerations will be different from those of someone who is sharing a smaller space with a partner or family.

Altar Height

When planning your altar, consider whether you would like to have a high or a low one. An altar on a shelf or dresser top might be considered a "high altar," and a "low altar" might be placed

A mirrored shrine creates an Internal Altar, honoring the sacred light within each of us.

on the ground or on a low table. Traditionally, high altars symbolized communion with the sky gods and heaven, while low altars related to the earth, the underworld and more subterranean qualities.[1] If your altar is dedicated to helping you explore hidden aspects of yourself, building it close to the ground and using many earth-colored objects and textures might be a way of visually representing your desire to dig down beneath the surface of your life. If, on the other hand, you want to transcend limitations and learn how to "fly" into the land of your dreams, you could make an altar on a high window ledge and drape it with light and airy gauze to give it a feeling of clouds and the sky.

Table Altars

Table altars are relatively easy to construct. Simply drape a colorful piece of silk, a scarf perhaps, over a coffee table – a small round or square table – and you have the beginnings of an altar. Alternatively, paint the table surface with special designs. You can also create a table altar by placing a board across two piles of stacked bricks. I once made a very effective altar by using two stacks of glass bricks, which had a beautiful luminescent quality, and placing a board on top that I had painted a soft shade of lavender. It made a light and lovely altar structure. Table altars can also be made on desks or on computer tables.

Wall Altars

If your home already has an alcove or small niche in the wall, it can be converted into a "high altar." An existing shelf can also be converted into an altar. I know a couple that stenciled the wall around a built-in shelf to give their home shrine a sacred feeling. Many home-furnishing stores carry small single shelves that attach to the wall. These are either ready-made or prepared for you to stain or paint in a way that is harmonious with your plans for your altar. Some of the most magical altars are handmade. By building a shelf for your altar you are infusing it with love and care that will continue to emanate from it for a long time.

Permanent Altars

If you have the time or inclination, you might decide to screen off a portion of a room or devote an entire room to your altar, or even build an additional area to house your home shrine. Over the years, a permanent altar will gain in strength and power that will continue to radiate and fill your entire home. In addition, the very nature of the altar's permanence lends a strong foundation to the prayers and meditations that are conducted there.

1 Turner, Kay, "Why we are so inclined . . .", *Lady-Unique-Inclination-of-the-Night, Cycle* 6, Spring 1983, p. 12.

This portable travel altar is self-contained – all the objects are inside a cloisonné box.

Portable Altars

Not everyone has a lifestyle that can include a permanent altar, so you might consider creating a portable altar that you can take with you through various moves or when you travel. When you are traveling you can personalize your hotel or guest room by bringing a portable altar with you. As a suggestion, decorate a small wooden box or any sturdy container and place a scented votive candle, some sticks of incense, crystals and other travel-safe objects within it. When you arrive at your new location, set up your portable altar on a shelf, dresser or night stand. Prop a beautiful card or photo up against the box, place the crystal and votive candle in front of the picture, and you have an instant altar. This traveling altar can help preserve a sense of the sacred wherever you are.

ALTAR *Construction*

After you have decided where to put your altar and the form it will take, you are ready for the construction stage. During this phase, you will gather your materials together, do whatever construction is necessary, select the objects which will be included, and decide how you will arrange them on the altar. This is a very important step in the creation of your altar, because the basic energy of your altar is established during its inception. The ongoing energy of your altar is dependent upon the care and thoroughness that you put into these preparatory stages.

Before you construct your altar, make an initial assessment of what you will need to do. Do you want to paint your altar area another color? Do you need to buy or build a table or special shelf? Are you going to use an altar cloth? Will you section off a portion of your bedroom with a screen or velvet curtain? Imagine viewing the altar from various vantage points in the room to sense the overall effect it will have. Notice how your altar will affect people walking through the room. Decide what overall feeling you wish to portray. Take your time with this step – you are setting the stage and the energy for everything which will follow.

Altar Cloth

Altar cloths are a very important part of the altar in many traditions. Although it is not essential, the altar cloth can provide a context for the rest of the altar. It represents the foundation that the altar is built upon, and the choice of fabric and color will greatly affect the entire structure. Altar cloths can add a depth of dimension to an altar. Texture and colors can be an additional area for personal expression and symbolic representation.

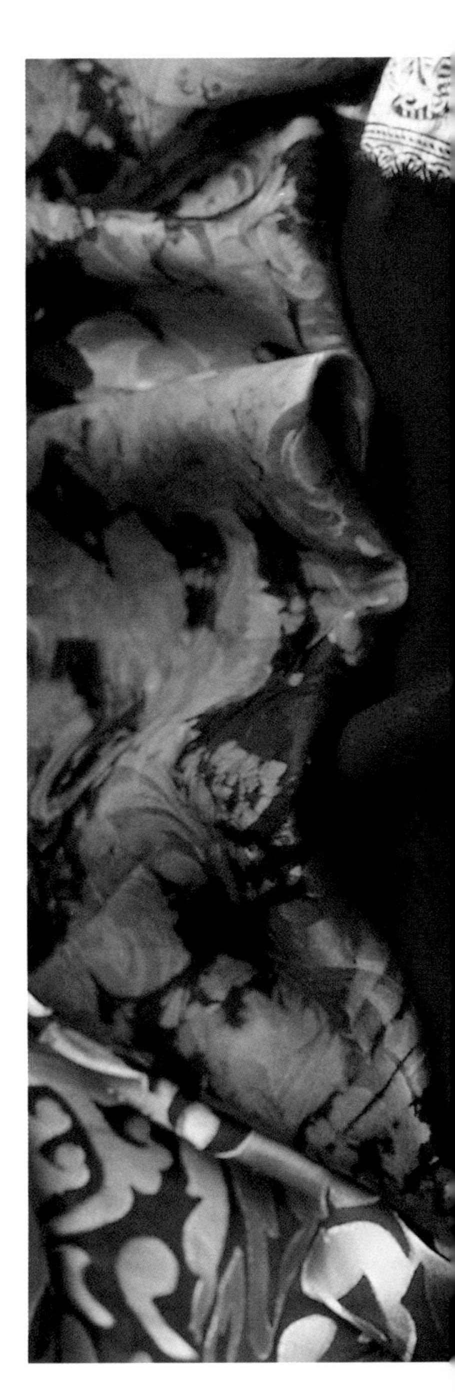

Indian silks make wonderful altar cloths.

Altar Objects

The selection of the objects that you use for your altar is important. Each item that you place on its surface should have meaning and significance for you. This is what generates the life force of your altar. When you gather the objects for your altar, take into account your altar's purpose, for this will help you decide what to use. For example, if you have an altar dedicated to love, you may choose to use items such as a velvet heart, fragrant potpourri and photos of friends and loved ones; all objects that reflect your overall intention for the altar. Your choices do not have to be permanent ones. Vibrant altars are continually evolving over time, and this change is what prevents them from becoming stagnant. So be adventurous. You may try some things and discover that they just don't work. Other things will turn out to be exactly right. This will be an ongoing process, for as your life and perspective change, the objects on your altar will change accordingly, too.

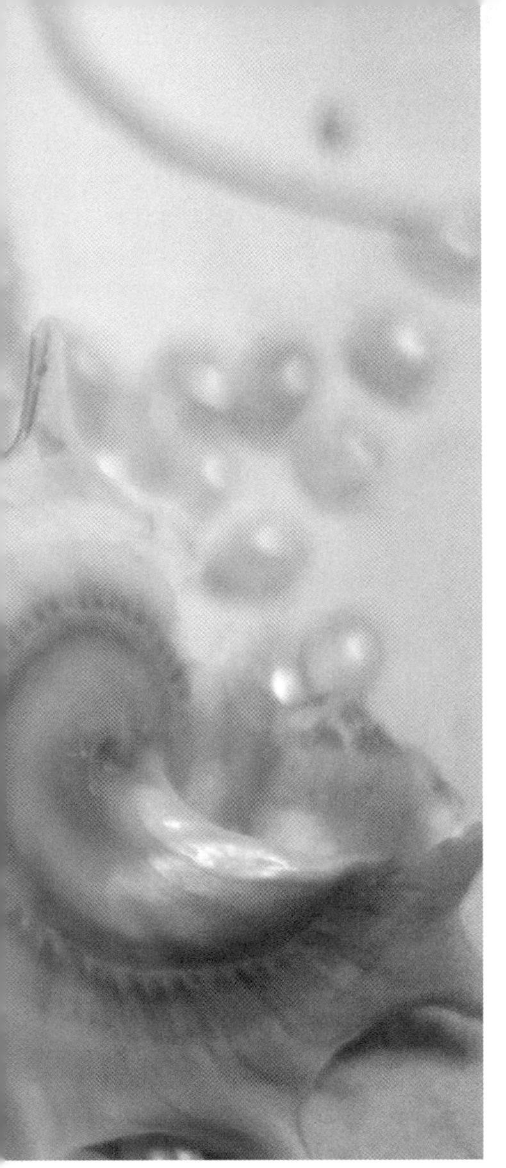

Shells on an altar can invoke the feminine energy of the sea.

Be sure to take into account the "essence" of each object you choose. An item's essence is influenced by a number of things: symbolism, the object's creator and origin and its physical substance. Many altar objects are steeped in symbolism. For example, a figurine, drawing or photo of a white dove represents peace for many people. Likewise, an oak tree often characterizes strength, and the moon universally symbolizes the feminine principle.

The essence of altar objects is influenced by their origin and substance as well as their mystic symbolism

Your altar object may also have a private meaning which is symbolic only to you. For example, if you had pleasant experiences as a child collecting seashells at the seaside, then a shell on your altar might personally represent joy. The essence of an altar object is also affected by the person who crafted or created it. If a happy person created the object on your altar, on a subtle level it will contain the cheerful feelings of the creator.

An altar object is also influenced by its origin. For example, an object that was made in the African jungle will have a very different energy from an object made in Switzerland. The African object may have an ancient and primal residual energy, while the Swiss object may have a subtle energy of clear mountain air.

Another influence on the energy of an altar object is the material of which it is made. A glass object has a completely different feeling from an object carved from wood. A clear glass item can have an energy that is cool, clear and precise, while a wooden object is more likely to be warm, earthy and natural. The color of your altar objects can also influence the overall feeling of your altar. An altar covered with items that are red, orange or yellow may feel stimulating and invigorating, while an altar with blue, lavender and purple items may feel soothing and relaxing.

Each piece that you choose for your altar is influenced by many factors. Take time to notice your feelings about every object to see if they are consistent with your intention for your altar.

Representation of the Divine

Every altar should have an object on it that represents the spiritual or Divine realms. At least one altar item should symbolically represent a dimension beyond the ordinariness of life. For one person this might be something from nature; for someone else it might be a picture of a spiritual teacher or an ancient god; for another it might be a small icon of Jesus or Mary. No matter what your personal spiritual beliefs, we each need to believe in something larger than ourselves, and this is centrally honored on an altar. Having an altar object that signifies a realm beyond the physical realm declares your altar to be a sacred space.

Objects from Nature

One way to bring the beneficial energy of the natural world into the home is by putting things from nature on your home altar. These objects symbolically bring the qualities of outdoors into our indoor environments. For example, a small pine cone on an altar can bring the feeling of the deep peace of the forest into your home, subliminally evoking the memory of soft moss and delicate flowers growing on the forest floor.

An object from nature can also inspire in you the feeling that you experienced when you first found it. Imagine walking through a mountain meadow filled with a wonderful sense of joy. On your walk you notice a small white, smooth pebble. You kneel down to pick it up. Placing that stone on your altar helps encourage those special sentiments that were occurring within you when you found the stone. Objects from nature can also have profound symbolic meaning. A rock can represent grounding and connection to the earth; a feather can symbolize higher aspirations; a gnarled stick can represent the wisdom and strength that comes with age; a rose might represent love.

Although the symbolism for natural objects varies according to custom and culture, here are some of the commonly held meanings for natural objects for your altar.

Natural Rocks and Stones

A natural stone on your altar not only suggests a grounding energy, it also brings the qualities of the area from which it came. For example, stones that have been smoothed and polished by the motion of the surf carry power from the depths of the ocean. Their spirit speaks of the surging changes of surf and sand. Stones found near roots of trees or along the base of cliffs have the spirit of the ancient land. Their spirit carries a richness of the dark loam of Mother Earth and her primordial secrets. Stones found in inland river beds and streams carry the flowing energy of water. Every stone carries the energy of its past, its composition and the area where it is found.

Natural stones can bring a grounding energy to an altar.

Polished Stones and Gems

Polished stones have been used on altars for thousands of years. This is partly because of their inherent beauty and their light-reflecting qualities, but also because over the centuries certain stones have been thought to represent certain characteristics. For example, amber represents protection, citrine symbolizes mental clarity, lapis represents spirituality and intuition, and quartz crystal symbolizes spiritual attunement.

Metals

Metals formed into shapes like goblets and swords have been used on altars not only for the value of skilled craftsmanship but also for the spiritual qualities of the metal. For example, gold on an altar represents the sun with its associated qualities of magnificence and expansion, silver symbolizes the lunar qualities of the Divine Feminine force and iron on an altar signifies strength and grounding.

Shells

Shells on an altar are usually associated with the feminine energy of the sea. Mother of pearl signifies the power of the sea and the moon. Pearls have been used on altars for thousands of years. They represent infinite compassion, protection and spiritual attunement. Synthetic pearls can be used, but they lack the depth of energy of natural pearls.

Bones and Horns

The bones and horns of an animal symbolize its spirit. For example, an elk bone on an altar can represent the strength and power of the elk. In Native American tradition, a buffalo skull is often placed on an altar to honor the gift of food and fur that the buffalo provided for their ancestral people. A deer antler on an altar can symbolize the bountiful qualities of deer.

Feathers on an altar symbolize the connection between heaven and earth.

Feathers

In many native traditions feathers are thought to be the connection between man and the Supreme Being. They symbolize the flight to the heavens. To the ancient Egyptians feathers represented the winds and the creator gods, Ptah, Hathor, Osiris and Amon. In Christianity, St. Gregory stated that feathers symbolize faith and contemplation and a quill signifies the Word of God.

Plants and Flowers

A living plant or cut flowers can bring a wonderful vital energy to your altar. Every plant and flower has its own unique properties. For example, the lily of the valley, which blooms in early spring, can signify new life and new beginnings. If you use living plants, make sure that they are healthy and thriving.

Dried Plants

Even when a plant or herb is dried, it still contains the essence of the living plant. A bowl of dried rose petals or a bunch of dried lavender can bring the natural world's energy into the home.

Herbs

Herbs are often placed on altars because of their associated qualities. For example, sage signifies purification, garlic often suggests protection and lavender can symbolize peace.

Fruit and Grains

Throughout history, fruits and grains have been placed on altars celebrating harvest and abundance. In addition, they are also similar to the symbolism of the egg because they contain the seed for new growth. For example, corn has been found on ancient altars and it has been suggested that it symbolized harvest, abundance, fertility and blessing. A shiny apple can signify health and vitality, and a peach has traditionally represented immortality and marriage.

Sometimes prepared food is placed on the household shrine. For example, in India, cooked food often is placed on the shrine before an image of a god. The food on the shrine becomes a focus for daily puja (a period of devotional prayer) which welcomes or invites the god into the home.

Tree Twigs, Branches, Pine Cones and Leaves

Ancient people throughout the world revered trees. From the Tree of Knowledge in Genesis, to Buddha gaining enlightenment under the Bodhi tree, to the Norse Tree of Life, to Native Americans calling the trees their "brothers" and "sisters," trees have represented a connection to the spiritual realms. Placing a part of a tree on your altar, such as a leaf or some bark, brings the special energy of the tree into your home. Every tree has its own unique energy. For example, the ginkgo tree symbolizes knowledge, ancient wisdom and longevity; the pine signifies purification, simplicity and forthrightness; and the oak tree represents strength and fortitude.

Sacred lotus flowers and floral offerings adorn this Thai Spirit Altar.

Aromatherapy: Essential Oils and Incense

The element of fragrance on your altar can bring a wonderful texture and richness to the overall energy. Placing aromatic flowers, lighting a single stick of incense or putting a small bowl of cedar chips, orange peels or pine needles on your altar can instantly create an uplifting feeling.

Throughout history various smells have been used for spiritual and therapeutic purposes. Over 2,000 years ago Hippocrates recommended the benefits of aromatics. The Bible also makes reference to healing with aromatic oils. In ancient times it was believed that scenting an environment with rare and special fragrances would attract gods and angels while at the same time repell negative forces.

Natural aromas carry the life force of the plant and give powerful energy to your altar

Modern research has discovered what many people have always known … that smell can affect the way you feel emotionally and can affect your energy level. More than any of our other senses, smell affects our emotional reactions. Our smell receptors are so sensitive that a single molecule of some substances is enough to excite one receptor ending; the human olfactory system can sense less than one-hundred-millionth of a gram of musk. If you have a special essential oil blend which you use only for your altar, then every time you smell it you will feel connected to the wonderful energy field created around your altar.

Fragrant flowers on an altar bring the senses alive.

There are numerous ways that you can add scent to your altar. However, any aroma on an altar should come from a natural source, as many people report allergic reactions such as headaches, sore throats, or even nausea due to chemical aromas. True essential aromatic oils are natural products created by the steam distillation of the plant or herb from which they are derived. Essential oils have a superior perfume, but more importantly, they also have the energy and spiritual properties of the plant. Essential oils don't have the constancy of synthetic smells, as they vary according to location, climate and soil conditions, but they carry the power and life force of the plant – which will be helpful to the energy that you are creating for your altar.

When adding fragrances to your altar, you might consider using essential-oil candles or naturally scented potpourri. Incense is also another wonderful addition to any altar. However, make sure it is high quality and not heavily perfumed with synthetic fragrance, as these types of incense can be effective for masking cigarette odor but have no place on an altar.

Vaporization is another excellent way to augment the energy of your altar through smell. A popular way to do this is to use a ceramic vaporizer. This has a small bowl on top which is filled with water to which a few drops of essential oil are added. A votive candle – which can last from four to eight hours – is placed in the cavity below the bowl of the vaporizer. The heat from the candle warms the water, which generates a pleasing, gentle flow of scent to the surrounding area. Vaporizers which use small night lights to generate heat are also available.

Some fragrances that you may find useful for your altar are frankincense and sandalwood for calming, releasing fear and spiritual clarity; lemon for uplifting, revitalizing and mental alertness; and pine for cleansing and purification.

Animal Symbols

Placing a symbolic representation of an animal on an altar is a practice that has been in use since ancient times. Traditionally, representations of animals were placed on an altar to help bring the qualities associated with the animal into one's life. For example, if a small carving of a bear or even a bear claw was placed on a home shrine, this was thought to call forth the protective strength and energy of the bear into the home.

The meanings of animals vary from culture to culture and from person to person. The most valid meaning is the one that intuitively feels right to you. Placing a symbolic representation of an animal on your altar can bring a deeper connection to the earth, as well as evoke the animal's special attributes.

A bear figurine on an altar represents strength and protection.

Images of Pets

In present times many people place a photo of a loved pet in a special place. Placing a picture of a favorite pet on a home altar helps remind us of all the good times shared with that animal and keeps a place in the heart for this special family member.

Religious Icons and Ancient Deities

Some people find great comfort in returning to the ancient deities of our collective past. Welcoming the energy of the deities of the past can sometimes fill a need not addressed by the religious systems of our times. A figurine or a painting or drawing of the deity can be placed on your altar as a reminder of the qualities that the deity represents. For example, a figurine of the Chinese Kwan Yin usually represents compassion and the nurturing mother; the Christian St. Francis of Assisi can symbolize purity, simplicity and kindness toward animals; and the Egyptian Isis often signifies the mother goddess and the inner feminine mysteries.

Sacred Objects

Whenever you place something on your altar that represents the spiritual ideals, you enter into a time-honored tradition because throughout history sacred or religious objects have been used for this purpose. There is power in objects that represent the Divine realms, so it is very important to examine the meaning that the sacred object has for you. For example, holy ash from a sacred fire can signify an open heart to the Creator. Prayer beads on an altar serve as a focus for prayers. A figurine of an angel with arms outstretched can indicate an opening to the heavenly realms. One woman placed a small calligraphy drawing painted by her revered Japanese Zen master on her altar. She felt it was a sacred object because her teacher's clarity and wisdom were evidenced in his painting. Sacred objects on an altar allow it to be truly a place where heaven and earth meet.

Color

The colors that you use for your altar can have a very strong influence on its overall energy. For example, if your altar is dedicated to peace, blues and cool colors are a better choice than stimulating warm hues. As a rule, the warm colors such as red, orange and yellow are revitalizing and active colors. They are great for an altar dedicated to taking action in life. If you have an altar dedicated to creativity and vitality, warm-toned colors are excellent. The cooler colors of green, blue and purple tend to be more relaxing and meditative, so these are good for an altar dedicated to peace and introspection.

A Kwan Yin statue placed on an altar signifies compassion.

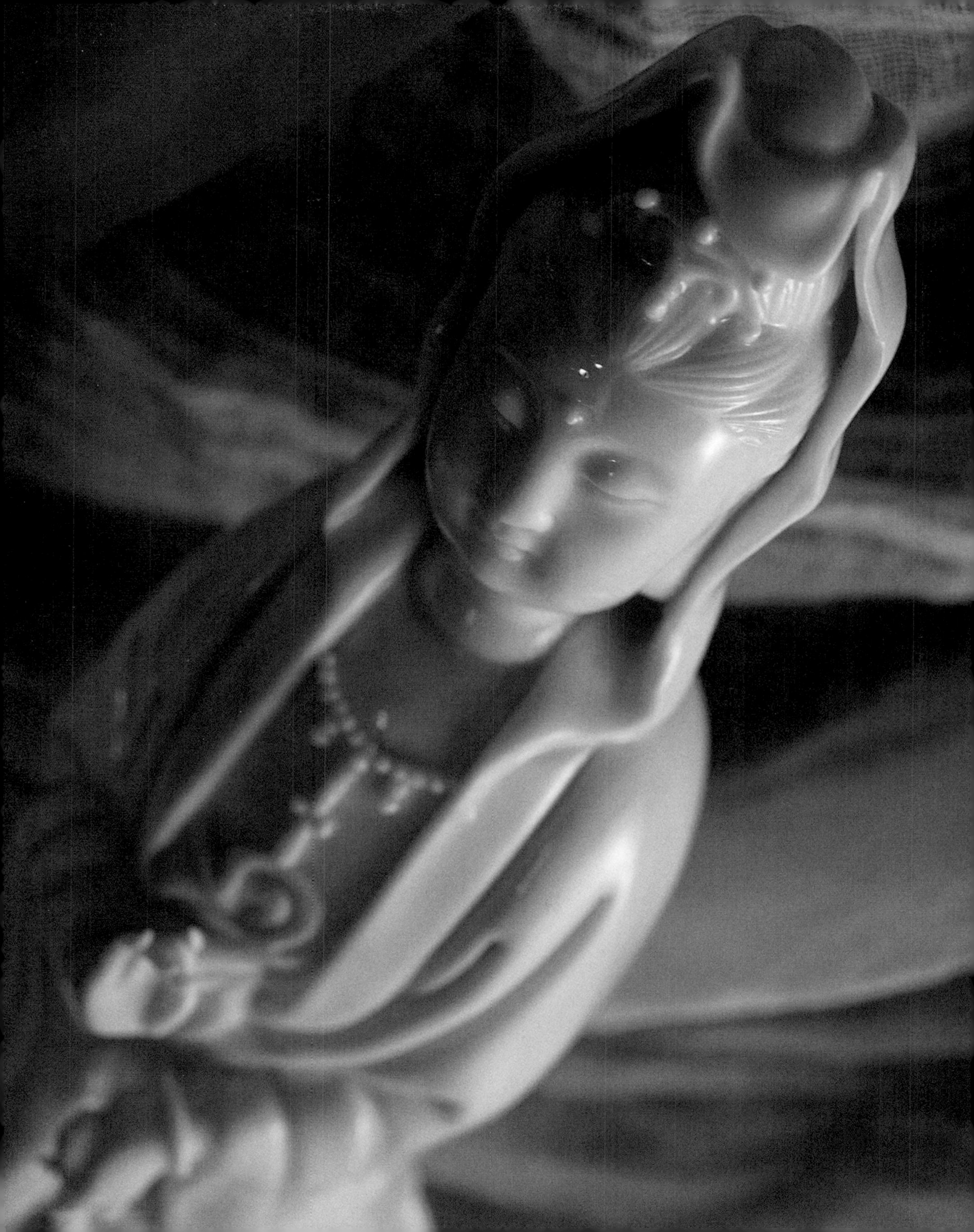

Symbolic Shapes and Patterns

Symbolic shapes and designs such as the circle or the cross provide a unique and profound catalyst for the expressions of human nature. They were used as early as Paleolithic times and have accompanied the expansion of civilization. Through the years these symbolic shapes have changed and grown in complexity, yet the themes have remained the same: connecting to spiritual realms and the Divine creative forces, fertility, birth and death. A symbolic shape on your altar serves as a focal point. It can convey deep meaning and help form a synthesis for all the various elements of your altar. Some shapes are universal, such as the circle, which usually represents wholeness and completion, and the cross (which preceded Christianity), which is a powerful symbol of the connection between heaven and earth.

Some symbolic shapes are cultural, such as the ankh, which is the ancient Egyptian symbol of life. Another cultural symbol is the yantra or mandala, which is a Hindu and Buddhist geometric diagram for meditation. In addition, often the cultural symbols from one's heritage can have a strong influence on the subconscious. Therefore, it is valuable to research your cultural heritage for the symbols that were meaningful to your ancestors. For example, if you are of Celtic heritage you might consider drawing some spirals to place on your altar, as spirals were revered by the Celts, who carved them into stones. The spirals were thought to indicate the creative forces of the universe.

A painted wheel of dharma – one of the eight sacred symbols of Buddhism.

Numbers

Since the beginning of time, numbers have been viewed as symbols which hold mystic significance. Clustering items on your altar in numerical groups can influence the energy in your altar. For example, placing three stones on it has a different feeling and energy than placing two. The three stones invoke the Trinity; two stones elicit the energy of the yin and yang. The following system is based on the Pythagorean system (on which modern numerology is founded).

One independence, new beginnings, oneness with life, self-development, individuality, progress and creativity.

Spirals carved into the ancient stones at Newgrange, Ireland.

Two balance of the yin and yang energies (the polarities) of the universe; self-surrender, putting others before yourself; dynamic attraction of one to another; knowledge comes from the balance and marriage of the two opposites.

Three the Trinity: mind, body and spirit; threefold nature of Divinity; expansion, expression, communication, fun and self-expression; giving outwardly, openness and optimism.

Four security and foundations; the four elements and the four sacred directions; self-discipline through work and service; productivity, organization, wholeness and unity.

Five feeling free, self-emancipating, active, physical, impulsive, energetic, changing, adventurous and resourceful; associated with travel and curiosity; the free soul, excitement and change.

Six self-harmony, compassion, love, service, social responsibility, beauty, the arts, generosity, concern and caring; relates to children, balance and community service.

Seven inner life and inner wisdom; a mystical number symbolizing wisdom, the seven chakras and the seven heavens; a symbol of birth and rebirth, religious strength, sacred vows, the path of solitude, analysis and contemplation.

Eight infinity, material prosperity, self-power, abundance, cosmic consciousness, reward, authority and leadership.

Nine humanitarianism, selflessness and dedicating your life to others; a symbol of universal compassion, tolerance and wisdom.

Ten completion as the number of fingers is ten; symbolic of return to unity.

Twelve 12 signs of the zodiac, 12 months of the year, 12 hours of the day and night, 12 Knights of the Round Table, 12 disciples; balance of spiritual realm and earthly realm.

Some other numbers in Pythagorean tradition were thought to have a special power and significance of their own:

Eleven intuition, clairvoyance, spiritual healing and other metaphysical faculties.

Twenty-two unlimited potential for mastery in any area, not only spiritual but physical, emotional and mental as well.

Thirty-three ancient mysteries; all things are possible.

Spiritual realms are often represented by candles on an altar.

Candles

The most universal items used on altars are candles. Since the earliest times candles were not only a source of light but also a powerful symbol of Spirit. Candlelight illuminating the darkness was believed to represent the spiritual spark in human beings that was fanned by the greater light of the Divine. Candles were also used on altars as a focus for concentration and meditation. When burning candles on your altar, remember never to leave them unattended.

A child's gift brings a special energy to an altar.

Tapers

Beautiful, elegant tapers create a wonderful focal point for your altar even when they are not lit. Tall slender tapers come in an array of colors and varieties: they may be hand dipped, rolled beeswax, creatively decorated or scented with essential oils. Make sure the wicks on altar candles are trimmed to prevent smoke. Use a candle snuffer to put out candles, or you may blow hot wax everywhere.

Votives

Tiny votive candles can make a lovely addition to your altar and are particularly useful for small altars and traveling altars. Glass containers for votives come in a variety of shapes and colors.

Glass-enclosed Candles

Glass-enclosed candles often used on home altars are called Novena candles and come with a particular saint's picture on them, with an inscription or with a picture of the cross or a prayer. When the candle is lit, the flame illuminates the inspirational picture on the glass surface. The custom for Novena candles originated in ancient Egypt. It is based on the idea that as you burn the candle you burn away difficulties, mistakes and problems, and begin anew. They are usually available in religious stores.

Photographs and Pictures

Photos bring a human quality to your altar. An image of your children, relatives or friends can help foster a positive connection to family. In addition, pictures of inspirational or spiritual people can help bring forth the qualities that they represent into the home. Having a photo of someone who inspires you on your altar can help you through difficult times, and can serve as a kind of spiritual beacon.

Special Gifts

Special gifts that you have been given through the years can bring a wonderful energy to a home altar. A meaningful gift carries all the love that accompanied it when it was given. A small child's brightly colored, hand-drawn birthday card makes a lovely adornment on an altar. By placing, perhaps, the special seashell that was a gift from a granddaughter or the diamond necklace that was a gift from a beloved great-aunt, you bring the wonderful memories associated with the gift onto your altar.

Ancestral Items

Traditionally, ancestral objects were placed on a home altar, and this tradition can have value in today's world. For example, a bit of lace from your mother, a carved wooden baby rattle from your great-grandfather, or the wedding ring of your grandmother on your altar can bring a recognition that you are a part of a rich and varied tradition that flows behind you and sails forth in front of you. (See Ancestral Altars on pages 70–74.)

Four Elements

Honoring air, water, earth and fire on your altar strengthens your connection with the natural world.

In cultures as varied as those of the ancient Greeks, early Celts and Native Americans, the four elements of air, water, fire and earth were honored. These comprised the essential elements of life, because without any one of these elements there would be no life on earth. By honoring the four elements you are acknowledging the most basic elements of nature. You are also honoring the four quadrants of your being, for in many traditions each element represents an aspect of human characteristics: Air – mental; Water – emotions; Earth – physical; and Fire – spiritual life force. (See the section on Medicine Wheel Altars on pages 58–61.)

Many traditions acknowledge the power of these elements by placing on the altar something that represents each of these elements. An empty bowl or chalice can represent the unseen, yet potent, element of air. Water may be represented by a vase filled with crystal clear water, or by a flower floating in a bowl. Fire could be symbolized by a candle or incense – even an unlit candle represents the element of fire. Earth might be symbolized by a stone, a container of sand or even a growing plant. By placing objects on your altar that represent these four elements, you are honoring the sacred cycles within your life and deepening your connection to the natural world.

Offerings

Generations ago offerings were made at altars to acknowledge and honor the gods and the creative forces of the universe. An offering was a presentation or gift – usually food and flowers or beautiful natural objects – made to a deity as an act of worship or sacrifice. The word "sacrifice," meaning to make holy, has its roots in Latin and it was considered a holy act to make offerings at the altar. In Egypt, the home altar was adorned with offerings of food, wine and flowers. In many Asian cultures, in a practice that continues today, the home shrine was gifted with daily offerings of rice, water, flowers and incense. In Native American tradition, offerings of tobacco, corn and corn pollen were made. In ancient Europe, altars were adorned with wine, grain and salt, and in Tibet perfumed water was used. Making an offering at your altar expresses gratitude for the bounty you have received and demonstrates an openness to the spiritual realms.

A traditional Chinese Buddhist altar. A feast for the senses, most Buddhist altars are adorned with offerings of fruit, flowers, incense and rice. These offerings express gratitude for blessings received and prayers for good fortune for the future.

THE *Purification*

After you have constructed the place for your altar and gathered together whatever objects you plan to use on it, you will want to do both a physical and a spiritual cleansing. For the physical cleansing, thoroughly clean the entire room or space in which your altar will be located. Clear out the clutter. Wash the windows. Sweep the floor. Make the entire room sparkle with radiant cleanliness and open a window to air out the room.

Next, purify the spiritual energy of the altar space. This can be done in a number of ways. You can burn incense or sage while saying prayers and gently dispersing the smoke around the altar with a feather. You can also purify the space with sound, either with drumming to dispel negative energy, or by using chimes, bells or rattles for the same effects. Continue the drumming or other sounds until you sense that all of the stagnant energy has been cleared from the space and you can feel that the air has a clear, light vibrancy to it. Chanting or singing in a room is also a powerful way to cleanse the spiritual energy there. You should also make sure that you and each altar object are cleansed and purified. (See the section on Purification on pages 131–136.)

Arranging the Objects on Your Altar

After you have purified yourself, the altar space and the things to be placed on it, it is time to decide how you will arrange the objects. This should be done in a caring and conscientious manner. You can arrange your altar either by using some logical placement plan or by relying on your intuitive or artistic feelings. Using the logical approach, you first decide what system you are going to use to determine where things will go. For example, you might logically decide to put smaller things in front and larger items at the back. Or if you are creating an Ancestor Altar, you might want to place most recent generational objects in front and the oldest at the back.

A second approach to deciding where you should put things on the altar is to use your intuition. To do this, simply place all of your chosen objects on the altar and then move them about until it just feels right. With this method, you are letting go of control and tuning in to your subconscious. When you move things about until their arrangement is truly pleasing to you, you might not have any conscious sense of why this is so, but at some deep level you will have achieved a meaningful balance.

Sage for burning, feathers for dispersing and a rattle to be used in an altar purification ceremony.

THE *Invocation*

Once the altar has been set up, it is time for its dedication ceremony. This is a kind of initiation or birthing rite for the altar. It can be as simple as lighting a candle and sitting silently for a few moments and allowing the spirit of the altar to fill your mind and heart. Or you could ring a bell and let your prayers follow the sound into the silence. You might finish your ceremony by saying a few words in prayer about your hopes and aspirations for the altar.

If this is to be a community altar, you might want to include the other members of your household, giving everyone a chance to say a few words, or perhaps simply sitting together in silence. This can be especially wonderful if the children who live in the home are included. They add a vigor that helps energize the altar. In addition, the ceremony is a meaningful experience which the children can look back on in later years.

There is nothing wrong with including family members even if they are not in complete accord with your feelings about the altar. Just tell them what it means to you and why you would like them to be included in the dedication ceremony. It is also fine if people who live in the home decline to be a part of the dedication ceremony. This can be a good opportunity to practice letting go and allowing things to happen in their own way.

The dedication ceremony invokes energy into the altar so that it will radiate out into your home and life like a small pebble dropped into the center of a deep pool. The ceremony helps your altar become a point of distillation for energy which can produce far-reaching effects in your whole life.

Here is an example of a prayer you could say at the time of the altar dedication:

May the Creator that dwells within all things bring blessings to this home and family.
May this altar be a constant reminder of the Divine spark that dwells in each of us.
Let joy, love, abundance, health and peace fill this home.

A Balinese bell used during the altar dedication ceremony.

THE *Preservation*

Once the energy of your altar has been established, you will want to preserve it so it stays fresh and renewed, always a source of strength and peace for you. There are a number of ways you can do this. The simplest, and certainly one of the most effective ways, is to meditate regularly at your altar. The power of your prayers and meditations infuses the altar with energy which shines out into the universe, magnifying what is in your heart into the world. This energy rebounds back to you, so that you feel filled with more vigor and joy. This two-way process can have an incredible effect on your life, even as it adds to the potency of your altar.

Another way of tending the energy of your altar is to keep renewable objects there, such as a bouquet of flowers, a single rosebud, fresh fruit, a living plant or spring water in a beautiful glass bowl. A small home fountain with moving water can also enliven your altar's energy.

It is valuable to have something on your altar which you always keep fresh. This is a potent symbol of the living connection that you have with your altar. By tending to the fresh, changing element that is on your altar, it becomes an ongoing part of your daily routine, not something which stands inert and unused in your life.

Another way to keep the energy of your altar alive is to give away something that is on it from time to time. Giving things from your altar keeps the energy flowing. An object from your altar is a very special sort of gift, because not only are you giving the physical item, but you are also gifting the spiritual energy it has absorbed from your altar. Whenever you give an altar object, it makes room for another one, which brings a new and fresh energy to your sacred space.

Using your altar can bring you closer to the cycles of the natural world and can align you with the rhythms of nature

Moving the objects on the altar around, changing elements when your heart and intuition tell you it is time to do so, will result in a living, loving relationship with your altar, which in turn will nourish you, bringing you fulfillment in all areas of your life. Your altar can be a solace for life's hurts, a center of joy and fun and a celebration for your triumphs. It can be a centerpoint to which you turn, to find your roots, to heal your wounds and to connect with the source of your soul's deepest truth.

The Creator's altar – infused with soft filtered sunshine, dappled light on the forest floor and a quiet moment.

THE *ceremony*

CEREMONIES *at the Altar*

Once you have created your altar, it becomes a place of power that attracts energy to it and radiates energy from it. It is a sacred space. The most effective altars are the ones that are used. Every time you use your altar in a ceremonial manner the energy field around it is strengthened. This, in turn, magnifies and deepens your devotion, contemplation, prayer or meditation time before your home shrine. When you use your altar regularly, it strengthens your spiritual path and infuses the most mundane aspects of life with a sacred sense of meaning.

Meditating at your altar strengthens your spiritual path and infuses the most mundane aspects of life with a sacred sense of meaning

You do not need to spend long periods of time before your altar for it to become a valuable asset to your home and life. Sometimes simply taking a moment of silence before the altar, placing a fresh bunch of flowers in a vase or lighting an altar candle can bring a deep feeling of sacredness and serenity. However, there may be occasions when you wish to spend more time at your home shrine. If this is the case, then there are four steps you might consider employing when using your altar.

The first step is Preparation. It is important to prepare yourself and your altar before you begin your meditation. The second is Focus. In this step, you use the altar as a focal point for your meditations and prayers. The third is Listening. It is during this period that you clear your mind and just listen to your innermost thoughts and to messages from spirit. The last step is the Completion phase, when you gain closure for your experience. These four steps will intensify the energy that emanates from your altar and will imbue it with vitality.

Candles are often used during ceremonies performed at an altar.

Preparation

Preparing for your time in front of your altar is important because it increases the potency of your meditations. The preparation period has three parts: the first is purification, the second is gaining clarity of your intention and the third is centering yourself. Carefully laying this groundwork will provide a foundation for each occasion that you use your altar.

Purification

Ideally you should purify the room, yourself and the altar each time before you use it. The time you invest in this process will directly influence the quality and effectiveness of your contemplation period at your altar.

Purifying the Room

Taking time to clean and clear energy in the room where your altar is placed will enhance your meditation. To gain the most value from your time before your shrine, it is helpful to clean the room that houses it. For example, a room stacked high with newspapers, an unswept floor and dirty coffee cups can be very distracting. Simply vacuuming, wiping down surfaces and picking up clutter is often sufficient to uplift energy in a room. There are times, however, when you may need to do a little more intensive clearing to enhance a room's energy. This is especially true if there has been an argument in the room, if someone in the household has been ill or if there is a general listless feeling in the home.

There are a number of ways to tell if the energy in a room is stagnant and needs an in-depth clearing. Colors often look physically dull and lifeless, sounds may seem muffled or you may feel a sense of shortness of breath, a lack of oxygen or that the air is heavy. It may even feel like you are trying to walk through honey. A room with stagnant energy is not conducive to contemplation. However, there are some very simple and easy techniques that anyone can do to uplift a room's energy, such as lighting a candle, ringing a bell or spreading the smoke of sage throughout the room. (See my book *Sacred Space*.)

An effective clearing technique is clapping your hands, because the sound of clapping can help to dispel sluggish energy instantly. Although the energy in a room may be cleared in different ways, such as using bells, drums and sage, clapping is a very potent method that anyone can employ. When you begin clapping in a room, start by doing it a few times at the entrance to the room or at the room's easternmost corner. As you clap, it is important that you keep your intention focused on the desired results you have for the room. Your intention will be magnified by the sound. Make sure that your body is relaxed in a comfortable stance. The sound should be clean, crisp and clear. If your clapping seems muffled or mushy, it usually means that the energy is still stagnant.

To disperse sluggish or dull energy, clap all the way from the floor up to the ceiling, with your arms spread apart after each clap. You are uplifting the energy of the room by clapping up toward the ceiling. Continue walking and clapping until you have circled the room. You can tell the room has been cleared because the colors will be more vibrant, as when the sun shines through the clouds after heavy rain, and the sounds in the room will be crisper and clearer. You may feel you can breathe more deeply and feel lighter and freer.

Purifying Self

After the room and environment around the altar have been cleaned and cleared, you may want to consider cleansing yourself. This can be done physically or spiritually, or both. Although it is not necessary to have a bath or shower before your time at your altar, being clean may feel better than sitting before your altar in dirty clothes, not feeling refreshed. A suggested purification ritual is to either soak in a bath to which a cup of salt has been added, or use salt as a scrub in your shower. Either way, the purifying qualities of salt will clean your energy field and prepare you for your contemplation time. After your bath or shower, rinse with cold water and your aura will glisten.

If you don't have the time or inclination to bathe in preparation for your meditation, then you might consider smudging yourself with sage smoke or misting yourself with aromatherapy as a method of spiritually cleansing. Smudging yourself is the Native American art of using smoking herbs in a ceremonial manner with the intent of self-purification. To create smudge smoke, first light a small bundle of herbs in a deep fireproof bowl. Traditionally sage is used, but other natural substances like cedar can also be used. When the herbs are ignited, gently blow the fire out and the bundle will continue to smoke.

To smudge yourself, cup your hands into the smoke and bring it toward your closed eyes. As you do this, say to yourself, *"That my eyes may see the truth."* Then toward your ears, *"That I may hear the truth."* Then do the same thing over your head, and say, *"That I may know the truth."* Move the smoke over the rest of your face and down your body, and over all your extremities. Lastly, bring the smoke in toward your chest, and say, *"That my heart might be pure and open."* This process will leave you in a cleansed, focused, energized state.

A bundle of sage placed in a deep fireproof pot to be used for smudging and purification.

A word of caution about smudging: herbs can continue to smolder for a long time even after they are apparently extinguished. So it is very important never to leave them unattended because of the risk of starting a fire in your home. When you have completed your smudge ceremony, tap the smoking herbs firmly in the bowl until the smoke has died out. Then place the herbs inside the bowl in the kitchen sink...just in case they are still smoldering.

Another way to purify yourself is to utilize the cleansing power of water. To do this, fill an atomizer with water and add a few drops of essential oil (pine, peppermint or lemon are all excellent for cleansing purposes). Gently spray yourself top to bottom with the intent that you are preparing and cleansing yourself for meditation.

Purifying the Altar

After you have cleansed the room and yourself, check over your altar and make sure that it is clean. An altar that is dusty or has dead flowers on it will not provide the kind of crisp, clear energy that is most beneficial for contemplation. If you have water on your altar, make sure it is clear and fresh. If there are plants or flowers, make sure that they are healthy and vibrant. If a candle has burned down, replace it. Look at the collection of items and their placement. Does your altar feel good to you? If not, is there anything that you want to remove or change? Periodically you might feel the need to rearrange the items on your altar. Doing this can help your altar to reflect your present needs and ideals rather than ones from the past, and can also uplift and purify the altar energy.

Let your intuition guide you as to what needs to be done

Purifying the Altar Objects

The objects that will be placed on the altar should also be cleansed so that they are free of any negative or stagnant energy. To do this, you should start by physically cleaning them to remove any dust, tarnish or other dirt. Some old objects have a patina of age which adds to their beauty and power, so this should not be removed. Let your intuition guide you as to what needs to be done.

Usually a periodic physical cleaning is enough to clear the energy of your altar objects. However, when you first place an object on a shrine it is important to do a more intensive purification. This can be done in a number of ways. Altar objects can be left in either sunlight or moonlight. Sunlight will burn away stagnant energy and will leave an energy that is radiant and bright. Moonlight is also effective but will leave its own gentler, more relaxed energy in an object. (Some things, such as photographs, might be damaged or become faded if exposed to direct

Altar objects that have been cleansed and purified strengthen the overall energy of an altar.

Crystals and polished stones bring a sparkling energy, healing and strength to an altar.

sunlight. In such cases, it is better to place them in a sunny location where the light is filtered and indirect.)

Objects can also be purified using smoke and fire. Fire-resistant items can be passed over a candle flame high enough to avoid soot marks. Other more perishable items can be passed through smoke from incense or sage. Exposing appropriate items to the elements – wind and rain and other weather – is a powerful way of restoring them to a fresh, clean state so long as they will not be damaged by this treatment. Rubbing objects with eucalyptus oil or sprinkling them lightly with salt are two other effective ways of clearing negative energy. Sprinkling or washing objects with energized water will also create a sparkling clean energy field around them. To create energized water, place ordinary water in a glass container and expose it to either sunlight or moonlight for a few hours. This will infuse the water with the energy of the sun or moon and make it useful for purification. You can also charge water by placing a quartz crystal in it for 24 hours.

Intention

After you have completed the purification stage, it is valuable to clarify your purpose or intention for your ceremonial time before your home shrine. As you focus your intention on a particular goal, your altar refines and intensifies this intention. Your focus then becomes like a laser beam cutting through the obstacles which have prevented you, in the past, from realizing your dreams. Amazing things can then be accomplished.

When you are certain about your intention, almost magically the forces of the universe coalesce to propel you toward your goal

Before any contemplation period in front of your altar, take time to clarify your specific purpose for that particular meditation. Where intention goes, energy flows. Some questions to ask yourself are: What is my overall intention for my meditation? What immediate and long-term results do I desire for this contemplation time? Is the layout and structure of my altar conducive to my intention? For example, if the focus of your quiet time before your altar is to increase your inner peace, but you have included photos of family members on your altar with whom you are angry, then the objects on the altar might not be the most harmonious for gaining peace. Focusing your awareness on your intention and on the results that you desire, through contemplation at your shrine, helps propel you in that direction. When you are certain about your intention, almost magically the forces of the universe coalesce to propel you toward your goal.

Centering

After you have cleansed and purified the energy around your altar and clarified your intention, take some time to quiet your thoughts. Unplug the phone and let other household members know what you are doing, so you won't be disturbed. Give yourself enough time so that you don't feel rushed. Your contemplation time should not be one more thing to cross off on your daily "to do" list. It is your time for yourself. It is sacred time; an oasis of simplicity and peace and communion with the realm of spirit. Your time before your altar will be richer and fuller as a result.

There are several ways that you can still your mind. A very simple method is to watch yourself breathe. Gently slowing the rate of your breathing while observing it usually brings a wonderful feeling of peacefulness. An additional breathing technique is to count each exhalation. Often, in a very short time, your mind becomes calm and focused.

Another way to still your mind is to pick one item on your altar and focus on it very intently. Place your entire attention on that one object. After a few minutes it will seem that the entire room becomes quieter. Sometimes a candle is excellent to use as a focal point. However, a flower, figurine or symbol on your altar all can be used with equally good results. Focusing on a special object on your home shrine can allow peaceful thoughts to replace distracting and disruptive ones.

Focus

After you have prepared yourself and your altar, you are now ready to use your altar as a centerpoint for contemplation. This is a sacred moment. You stand at a threshold between two worlds. Sit or stand before your altar. Focus your awareness on it. (You can do this with your eyes either open or closed.) Rather than concentrating on one part of it, embrace your altar in its totality. Allow its energy and feeling to encompass you. Imagine that there is a line of energy between you and the entire altar and that the altar is a point of convergence for the forces of the universe. Your altar thus becomes a distillation point for communing with the Divine. At this point you may consider doing an active type of contemplation such as prayer, mantras, affirmations, deep concentration or visualization, all of which allow you to focus your mind and deepen your awareness of inner spiritual realms.

Prayer

One form of focused contemplation is prayer. The altar helps to magnify and intensify your prayers. When you pray, the words you use are less important than your sincerity. As you sit before your altar, you can speak or sing your prayers out loud. You can also invoke the Creator without words, directly from your heart. You do not need to be eloquent or explain yourself. Be real. Be honest. Be sincere. Often the best way to pray is to be focused and yet relaxed at the same time. A prayer that I often use is "Thy will and my will be one," so that whatever is received is in harmony with the Creator's plan for your life.

You can also pray for guidance from your personal spiritual helpers, who are always lovingly watching over you. A simple way to do this is to say, "May the spirits, guides, ancestors and angels that have gathered in peace, bring love and guidance. I give thanks for the help that is given. May what is received be for the good of all."

One type of spirit helper is the spirit guide. Guides are spiritual beings who have been on the earth before in a physical form, but are now in the heavenly realms. You have a guide...everyone does. Spirit guides understand the difficulties and challenges of living on earth and offer valuable and loving support. They are excellent to call upon if you are struggling with earthly issues.

Your ancestral spirits are another type of spirit helper you can call upon. Native cultures throughout history have used altars to honor and connect with the spirits of their ancestors. Those ancient people believed that ancestral spirits were always nearby and ready to offer assistance, especially in times of need. Ancestral spirits are especially good to call on if you are dealing with family issues.

In native cultures, the altar is also used as a place to invoke spirit animals for guidance and assistance. In these earth-based cultures, there is the belief that every person is spiritually aligned with a particular animal. When called, in times of need, the collective spirit of that animal is thought to bring help. If you do not know what your spirit animal is (also called "totem animal" or "power animal" or "animal ally") you can say, *"I call upon the energy and power of my spirit animal"* and leave the type of animal unnamed until you gain the understanding of what your spirit animal is. Even if you are not consciously aware of your spirit animal, this simple request will ensure their assistance. (To learn how to find your spirit animal, read my book *Quest*.)

During your prayers, you can also call upon any of the spirit animals to assist you. For example, if you need to have an overview of your life, you might call upon the Eagle Spirit, which has the ability to view people and situations from a detached and logical point of view. You might say, *"Brother Eagle, help me see my world with your clarity."* (See appendix for information about the symbolism of animals.)

One of the most powerful and easily accessible spirit helpers is the angel. I believe that each person has a personal guardian angel, and one of the fastest ways to gain assurance, love and support at your altar is to call upon your angel. Your special angel is only a thought away, and when you send forth a prayer to your angel your prayer is heard. To increase the presence of angels in your life, place an angel picture or figurine on your altar.

A statue or figurine of an angel on an altar can increase awareness of the angelic realms.

Mantra

An active form of meditation is the use of a chant or a mantra. A mantra is a word or words that have significance either from their sound or from their meaning. When you continually repeat a mantra, a remarkable energy begins to build. An excellent mantra to use is the ancient Sanskrit word "Om." Om (also spelled Aum) in Buddhism and Hinduism is considered a sacred syllable. It is believed to be the sound that represents the spoken essence of the universe. Om is used in affirmations and blessings. Often, after a few moments of chanting Om, a person will feel a sense of peace and relaxation. There are many traditional chants that you can use. However, creating your own chant or repeating a word such as "loving" or "joy" can also produce excellent results.

Affirmations

Another form of active meditation before your altar is the use of affirmations. An affirmation is repeating a positive thought over and over again, either aloud or silently, to allow its message to imprint on your subconscious mind. An example would be to repeat to yourself these words: "I am a valuable person," or "I am strong, healthy and well." Your altar can serve as a focus point to magnify your affirmations. To use your altar in this way, first focus on the altar item that is most strongly aligned with your desired results. For example, if you want more love in your life, focus on a rose (a symbol of love) on your altar and say your affirmation – perhaps "I am a lovable person."

Concentration

Contemplation can also take the form of highly focused concentration. To use this method, choose an object which has significance for you. This might be a mirror, the flame of a candle, some shiny or lustrous object, or a crystal ball. Place this object on your altar and stare intently at it. Imagine that you are concentrating at some point beyond the surface and into its depths. Feel that you are merging with this item until there is no division between it and you. This type of contemplation can allow you to enter into a profound altered state of consciousness.

Creative Visualization

There is a remarkable creative power that dwells in your mind. Creative visualization, which is the act of visualizing the results that you desire in life, activates this natural ability. To use creative visualization, place an object on the altar that represents what you wish to create in your life. Look at this, close your eyes and visualize yourself achieving your desires. For example, if you want to become a healer, place a healthy plant on your altar to represent this desire. Focus your attention on the plant, close your eyes and visualize yourself working with people in a healing capacity.

Listening

Often the most profound revelations and insights emerge during the quietness that follows your active contemplation period, while you are sitting in stillness before your altar. It is in the silent moments of life that remarkable inner knowing can occur. This is the time to be open and listen to the voice within yourself. Accept. Receive. Breathe. Observe. Just be. It is during the tranquil moments, while sitting before your altar, that you may receive an inspirational thought or an inner knowing will unfold. Spiritual insight doesn't often come as an instant realization but rather as a gentle emerging awareness. To encourage this type of contemplation, be conscious of the thoughts that float through your mind. These can provide a deep understanding about your life and your future.

While you are trying to be open and listen, if you find that your mind is filling with mental chatter about seemingly unimportant things, or if you have difficulty ignoring distractions, just say to yourself, "And this too." This simple statement allows you to acknowledge the mental diversion, so you can let it go. What you resist persists, so instead of resisting distractions, simply acknowledge them to let them go. In addition, if you find yourself becoming distracted, just keep bringing your focus back to your altar. Choose one object on your altar that you feel a close connection to and use it as a focal point. The object can help bring you back to the sense of closeness to spirit and serenity that is so helpful.

Watching or observing your thoughts is another excellent centering exercise. To do this don't try to stop your thoughts, but at the same time, don't encourage them. Just be aware of what you are thinking. This may take a bit of practice, but it is an excellent exercise to begin any contemplation.

Even a tiny corner in the garden can provide a tranquil space for contemplation.

Completion

Endings are as important as beginnings, so it is valuable to bring your time in front of the altar to a sacred completion. Doing this provides a sense of grounding so you are ready to face your day with renewed confidence. A gracious act of closure can be taking a moment to give thanks. You may want to give thanks to the Creator, your spiritual helpers and your higher self for whatever insights or other benefits you have gained from your time with your altar. Gratitude is one of the best ways of enhancing your experience and renewing the spiritual energy of the altar.

Some people gain a sense of completion by spending a few moments noting their thoughts and insights in a special journal which they keep as part of their altar space. This can be a very helpful way of synthesizing and recording the learning which has taken place. Also, it can be interesting to look back over time and review how the time at your altar has enhanced your life. Recording your hopes and intentions and then seeing how they have manifested in various ways in your life can be a tremendously affirming process.

At the culmination of your contemplation, rearrange and straighten the elements and objects of the altar. Although it is not necessary, some people like to drape cloths over photos or statues, or even over the entire altar. You will want to extinguish any candles which have been burning (unless you are burning a safely contained flame). This time of rearranging the altar's objects and completing the ceremonies which you have conducted accomplishes two things. It intensifies and sets the energy field that you have created for yourself in your meditation so that the benefits will stay with you. It also intensifies and sets the energy field of the altar itself. An altar that is regularly used in this way becomes more viable and effective over time.

Expressing gratitude at your altar during your contemplation is one of the best ways of renewing your spiritual energy

When you use the four steps of Preparation, Focus, Listening and Completion, you create a full circle. Each step strengthens and empowers the time that you spend with your altar. Following are some examples of how these four steps can work together, when more than one person is using the altar toward a particular goal.

Using the Four Steps

New Home Altar

Moving into a new home is an excellent time to create and use an altar. This can serve two purposes: it can help cleanse the energy of the previous tenants and it can call in fresh, revitalizing energy for the new occupants in the home.

Preparation: Invite friends and family to join you in the creation of this altar. Ask each person to bring something that symbolizes the blessings that they have for you and your family in your new home.

Clean and purify the room where you are going to create your altar, and also cleanse yourself, your friends and your family. Sage is good to use for a new home altar because of its cleansing properties. Make sure that the designated area for the altar is clean, the altar cloth (if you are using one) has been laid and the central object for the altar has been chosen. Then take a moment to hold an intention of what results you desire for your future in your new home.

Focus: Light a candle and ask each person to step forward, stating aloud their intention for the new home. They should then each place their object on the altar.

Listening: Take a moment of stillness to be open to spirit. Everyone should sit quietly and close their eyes, or stand quietly in front of the altar. If anyone intuitively receives any guidance for the family in their new home, this is the time to share it.

Completion: Extinguish the candle. Give thanks. Share a meal. Celebrate. The energy from the house ceremony will continue to radiate from the altar in the years ahead.

New Year Altar

The new year is an excellent time to sow spiritual seeds for the coming twelve months. Your altar can be an exceptional place to renew your personal energy and your home's energy for the next year. This ceremony can be done at the winter solstice, which is the celestial beginning of the new year, or it can be done on January 1st, which is society's beginning of the new year. (If you are of Chinese descent, you may want to celebrate Chinese New Year, which begins on the second new moon after the winter solstice. Or your faith may dictate a suitable date in your religion's calendar.)

Overleaf: Objects on a New Year Altar – the eggs represent a new beginning, and words of affirmation are written on rice paper.

Preparation: Decide who you wish to include in the ceremony. Will there be other occupants of the home, or will you do this ceremony by yourself? If others are to be included, ask them to write down their thoughts and wishes for the coming year. Do this yourself as well. Become very clear about your intentions for the coming year.

Purify the room, the altar, yourself and the others who are participating. You might want to take an atomizer filled with water that has been exposed to the sun and gently spray everyone and the room as a part of your cleansing ceremony. This is also a good time to re-energize your entire altar by taking everything off it, cleaning and cleansing each object and then carefully placing each item back on your shrine.

In your New Year Altar the centermost object should symbolize the Divine. In addition, it is beneficial to place an object or objects associated with new beginnings, such as seeds or egg-shaped objects, on your altar. Also, place an item or items that symbolize individual and group wishes for the year ahead.

Focus: As you sit before your altar, each person should visualize the coming year unfolding in grace, beauty and strength. This is a good time to send forth prayers for the future. These can be said out loud or they can be silent prayers.

Listening: Be still and open to receive inner messages regarding the months ahead and how to best stay in balance. If you are doing this with a group, you may also want to include time to share any insights that were received during this listening phase.

Completion: Give thanks for the blessings that you have received and will continue to receive. Blow out any candles which you have lit, and spend a few moments letting the blessings and the pure energy of the new year fill you with fresh energy and hope for the times ahead.

The Altar Within

Your home altar can transform private space into sacred space, which brings artistry, respect, love and spirit into your environment. It can be a remarkable metaphor for the beauty and harmony that dwell at the center of your existence. The enhancement of personal power and spiritual growth, which result from creating and using an altar, can change your life in a positive way so that your life becomes a kind of altar, a beacon of light beaming love and peace to all.

The beauty and peace of this woodland glade are a part of our natural birthright. They represent an essential harmony that altars may help us to reclaim.

appendix

MEANINGS OF *Altar Objects*

The meanings for altar objects change from culture to culture. They also vary person to person. The most valid meaning is the one that intuitively feels right to you. Below is a partial list of different objects you may want to use on your altar with their associated meanings. This is by no means a definitive guide, for the realm of symbolism is vast and diverse, but it does give a brief overview of numerous items you can put on your home shrine.

Religious Items

CHALICE – Holy Grail, fulfillment

HOLY ASH – from a sacred fire or from cremation of a holy person

MEDICINE BUNDLE/MEDICINE BAG – bundled collection of sacred objects

PRAYER BEADS/MALA – many religions use these as a focus for prayers

PRAYER FLAGS – symbolize and carry prayers on the wind to the heavens

PRAYER STICK – stick decorated with feathers and beads; prayers made visible

RELIGIOUS BOOKS – either to read a bit every day or to energize altar

TIBETAN PRAYER WHEEL – hand-held windmill inscribed with sacred verses

YANTRA/MANDALA – sacred geometric design used as aid for meditation

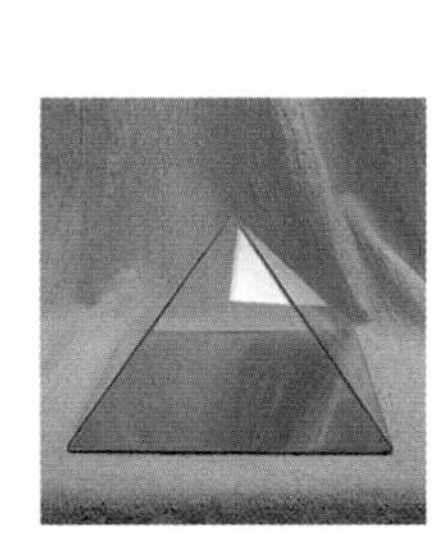

Symbols, Shapes and Patterns

ANKH – ancient Egyptian staff of life

CADUCEUS – two intertwined serpents representing healing

CIRCLE – completion, wholeness

CORNUCOPIA – abundance, plenty

CROSS – Christianity, intersection of heaven and earth

DOOR, GATEWAY – transition to other realms

EGG – new beginnings, regeneration

EYE – inner life, inner light

FEATHER – unity with Creator

HAND – creation, power, blessings

KEY – opening inner realms

KNOT – bonding, cohesion, unity

LADDER – ascending from earth to the heavens

PENTAGRAM – five-pointed star of harmony and balance

PYRAMID – ancient mysteries, revelations

RAINBOW – connection to the Creator, oneness

SPIRALS – movement of energy and the universe

SQUARE – solidity, foundation, earth, order

STAR – the heavens, great attainment

SWORD – truth, clarity, focus

TRIANGLE – divine trinity, path toward higher unity

WHEEL – movement, change, endless circle of existence

Religious and Ancient Deities

Chinese and Japanese

BUDDHA – purveyor of compassion

CONFUCIUS – wise teacher, often seen on household shrines

DAIKOKU – god of abundance

KWAN YIN – compassion, nurturing mother

Christian

JESUS – the savior

ST. FRANCIS OF ASSISI – purity, simplicity, patron saint of animals

ST. CHRISTOPHER – patron saint of travelers

VIRGIN MARY – compassionate mother

Egyptian

HORUS – falcon-headed sky-god and hero

ISIS – mother goddess, inner feminine mysteries

OSIRIS – powerful fertility god

RA – sun god

THOTH – lord of the moon

Greek

APOLLO – sun god, god of light and music

ATHENA – goddess of wisdom

EROS – god of earthly love

HERMES – messenger of the gods

POSEIDON – god of the sea

ZEUS – king of the gods

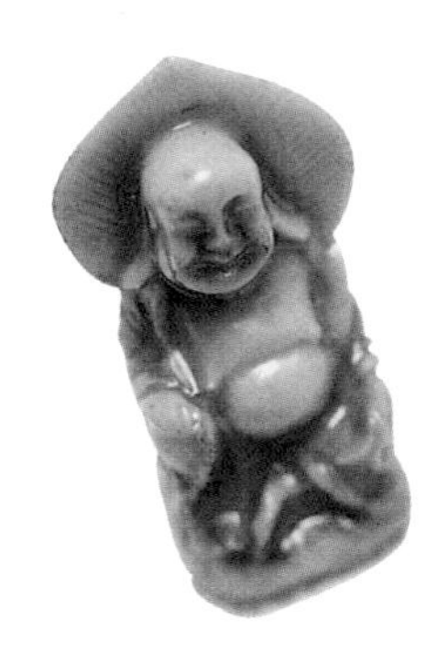

Hindu

DURGA – mother goddess

GANESHA – god to help overcome all obstacles

HANUMAN – loyalty, religious devotion, courage

KRISHNA – an incarnation of Vishnu

SHIVA – god of destruction which ensures rebirth

VISHNU – supreme being

Norse

FREYA – goddess of fertility and birth

ODIN – god of wisdom and of war

THOR – god of thunder

Roman

JUPITER – king of the gods

MERCURY – messenger of the gods, god of commerce

MINERVA – goddess of wisdom

NEPTUNE – god of the sea

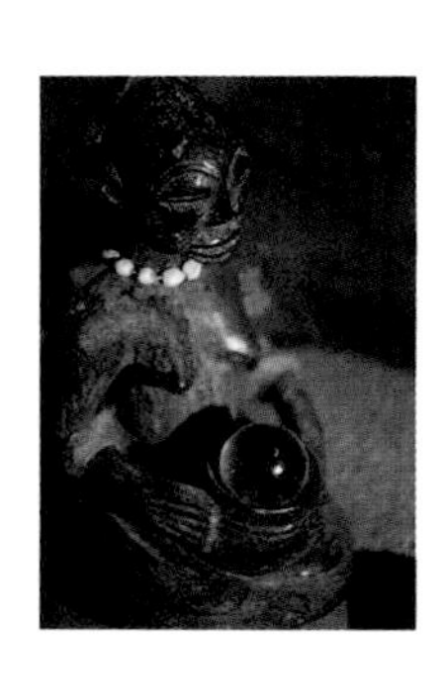

Offerings

ASHES – purification, regeneration
CORN – harvest, abundance
FLOWERS – emblem of the Divine
FRUIT – feminine spirit, harvest
GRAIN – prosperity, renewal
HONEY – sweetness of the gods
RICE – good fortune
SALT – purification, resurrection
TOBACCO – connection to spirit world
WATER – cleansing, spiritual attunement
WINE – blood of life, eternal life
WREATHS – cycle of life

Offering Containers

BASKET – wholeness, divine feminine principle
BOX – the unknown, containment
CALDRON – abundance, goddess power
CHALICE/ CUP – communion, Holy Grail, abundance
JAR/POT/URN/VASE – primordial feminine principle, Mother Earth

Sacred Sounds

BELLS – carry you past your mind into your soul
CHANTS – help you enter into altered states of consciousness
CHIMES – bring an energy of clarity
DRUMS – connect us to primordial sound of the mother's heartbeat
FLUTES – connect with the spirit
GONGS – powerful purveyor of messages from the unconscious
RATTLES – connection to the earth, relaxing, altered states of consciousness

Polished Stones and Gems

ADVENTURINE – healing
AGATE – success, happiness
AMBER – protection, healing
AMETHYST – compassion, clairvoyance
AQUAMARINE – harmony
BLOODSTONE – healing, physical straightening
CARNELIAN – physical grounding
CITRINE – mental clarity
DIAMOND – remarkable strength, fortitude and clarity
EMERALD – spiritual healing
FLUORITE – mental attunement, calming
GARNET – physical strength, assertiveness
JADE – healing, wisdom
LAPIS – spirituality, intuition, royalty
MALACHITE – psychic power, healing, cleansing
MOONSTONE – emotional balancing, lunar qualities
OBSIDIAN – grounding
ONYX – grounding
OPAL – emotional clarity
PERIDOT – mental and physical healing, rejuvenation
QUARTZ CRYSTAL – spiritual attunement
RUBY – strength, health and spiritual passion
SAPPHIRE – devotion and spirituality
SELENITE – dreaming skills, intuition, meditation

SUGALITE – higher spiritual realms

TOPAZ – expansion, knowledge

TOURMALINE – purification, healing

TURQUOISE – healing, balancing

Metals

BRASS – brightness, boldness

COPPER – transformation

GOLD – solar metal, magnificence and expansion

IRON – grounding, strength

SILVER – ruled by moon, receptive feminine force, intuition

Plants and Flowers

CHRYSANTHEMUM – introspection, meditation, longevity

CROCUS – new beginnings

DAFFODIL – childlike joy, laughter

DAISY – innocence, happiness

IRIS – delicate sensuality

JASMINE – beauty, joy

LILY – purity, perfection

LILY OF THE VALLEY – spring and new life

LOTUS – enlightenment, rising above darkness into light

MARIGOLD – longevity

NARCISSUS – divine love, good luck and fortune

PRIMROSE – finding joy in adversity

ROSE – love

SUNFLOWER – optimism, joy

TULIP – vitality, sensual love

VIOLETS – precious, tender, secretive

Shells

MOTHER OF PEARL – feminine energy, power of the sea and the moon

NAUTILUS – the divine proportion of all things

PEARL – infinite compassion, protection, spiritual attunement

Herbs

GARLIC – protection

GINGER – potent vitality

PEPPER – stimulation

PEPPERMINT – refreshment, cleansing

ROSEMARY – potent, vigorous

SAGE – purification, cleansing

TOBACCO – sacred Native American plant

Fruit and Grains

APPLE – health, vitality

CORN – harvest, abundance, fertility, blessing

MUSTARD SEED – faith

PEACH – immortality, marriage, tenderness

POMEGRANATE – fertility, unity of diversity

WHEAT – abundance, harvest

Twigs, Branches and Leaves

ALDER – joy, expansion

APPLE – health, vitality

ASPEN – open to change

BIRCH – emotional healing

CEDAR – purification, courage, strength
ELM – stateliness, grace, compassion
EUCALYPTUS – cleansing, vitality
FIR – purification, nobility
GINKGO – knowledge, ancient wisdom, longevity
MAGNOLIA – opening to the abundance in life
MAPLE – expansive beauty, grace
OAK – remarkable strength and fortitude
OLIVE – peace
PINE – purification, simplicity, forthrightness
SYCAMORE/ LONDON PLANE TREE – expansion, protection
WILLOW – healing emotions and loss

Essential Oils and Incense

BASIL – uplifting, clarifies thought processes
BERGAMOT – uplifting, yet calming
CEDARWOOD – relaxing
CHAMOMILE – soothing and calming,
EUCALYPTUS – invigorating, cleansing, purifying
FENNEL – relaxing, warming, calming
FIR NEEDLE – refreshing, cleansing
FRANKINCENSE – calming, releasing fear, spiritual clarity
GERANIUM – balancing mood swings, harmonizing
JUNIPER – purifying, stimulating
LAVENDER – calming, soothing, relaxing
LEMON – uplifting, mental alertness
LEMON GRASS – stimulating, cleansing, purifying
LIME – invigorating, refreshing
MANDARIN ORANGE – uplifting, refreshing
MARJORAM – very relaxing, anxiety reducing
MYRRH – strengthening, inspiring
NEROLI – stress reducing, calming
ORANGE – uplifting, refreshing
PATCHOULI – inspiring, sensuous
PEPPERMINT – stimulating, cleansing, refreshing, invigorating
PINE – refreshing, cleansing, stimulating
ROSE – emotionally soothing, loving
ROSEMARY – stimulating, cleansing, invigorating
SAGE – cleansing, purifying
SANDALWOOD – spiritual attunement, soothing, helps release fear
SPEARMINT – refreshing, stimulating
THYME – stimulating, strengthening, activating
VETIVER – relaxing, regenerating
YLANG YLANG – soothing, sensuous

Animal Symbols

land animals

ANTELOPE – swiftness, speed, agility
APE/MONKEY – protection, family, ingenuity
BADGER – ferocity, courage, tenacity
BEAR – healer, strength, stamina, introspection, protection
BEAVER – persistence, group harmony, productivity
BISON/BUFFALO – abundance, courage, determination

BULL – strength, stubbornness, determination, power, fecundity
CAT – independence, cleverness, mystery
COUGAR/MOUNTAIN LION – silent power, self-confidence
COW – fertility, contentment
COYOTE – cleverness, playfulness, family orientation
DEER/STAG – grace, fertility, regeneration, strength
DOG – loyalty, protection, faithfulness
DONKEY/ASS – surefootedness, determination
ELEPHANT – patience, royalty, power
ELK – stamina, nobility, warrior spirit
FOX – camouflage, cunning, quickness
GIRAFFE – farsightedness, reaching goals
GOAT – surefootedness, reaching new heights
HIPPOPOTAMUS – birth, the great mother
HORSE – power, freedom, grace
LEOPARD – valor, elusiveness, hidden knowledge
LION – self-confidence, radiant power
MOOSE – balance, gentleness yet strength, majestic yet awkward
MOUSE – discovery, attention to detail, invisibility, scrutiny
OTTER – joy, playfulness, receptivity
PANTHER – intuition, inner power
PIG/BOAR, SOW – courage, cunning
POSSUM – strategy, stillness
RABBIT/HARE – fertility, intuition, quick thinking
RACCOON – adaptation, creativity, dexterity
RAM/SHEEP – staying in balance in precarious situations
RAT – cunning, assertiveness, intelligence
RHINOCEROS – ancient wisdom
SKUNK – self-respect, self-confidence, courage
SQUIRREL – energy, intelligence, discovery
TIGER – strength
WEASEL – stealth, cunning
WOLF – family, loyalty, strength

aquatic animals

DOLPHIN – joy, peace, sacred messenger, wisdom
EEL – grace, power
FISH – fertility, Christ light, abundance
OCTOPUS – ancient wisdom
SALMON – spiritual knowledge, determination
SEAL – grace, joy
TUNA – ancient power, strength
WHALE – trust, faith, balance, harmony

winged creatures

BAT – sacred mysteries, the great mother, transformation, primordial darkness, rebirth, initiation
BLACKBIRD – mystic ancient wisdom, inner knowledge, hidden insights
BLUE BIRD – joy, confidence, gentleness, modesty, contentment
BLUE JAY – courage, speaking one's truth, adaptability
CANARY – sacred sounds, sensitivity, opening of throat chakra
CARDINAL – confidence, vitality

CHICKADEE/TITMOUSE – cheerfulness, joy, endurance, fearlessness
CHICKEN – service, sacrifice, fertility
COCK/ROOSTER – sexuality, alertness, fertility, enthusiasm
CRANE – longevity, focus, discipline, vigilance
CROW – magic, mystery, great intelligence, messenger from realm of spirit
DOVE/PIGEON – peace, feminine energies, maternal instincts, gentleness, love
DUCK – emotional balance, domestic harmony
EAGLE – illumination, spirit, power, creation
FALCON/KESTREL – speed, grace, power, absolute determination to reach a goal, achievement
GOOSE – sacred quests, transformation, mystical journeys, community
HAWK – visionary, strength, messenger from spirit, decisiveness
HERON – dignity, self-reliance, individuality, patience
HUMMINGBIRD – joy, tireless energy, delight, hope
KINGFISHER – peace, prosperity, love, luck

OSTRICH – grounded, balance between ancient wisdom and practicality
OWL – wisdom, visionary, magic, feminine energies, ancient secrets
PARROT – optimism, joy, confidence
PEACOCK – magnificence, sacred protection, dignity, self-confidence
PELICAN – generosity, self-sacrifice, buoyancy, prosperity
RAVEN – messenger from spirit, ancient mysteries, shape shifting
ROBIN – new beginnings, joy, activation of creative inner force, happiness
SEA GULL – emotional balance, communication, spiritual messengers
SPARROW/WREN – cheerfulness, love of home, fertility, boldness
STORK – fertility, balanced home, new beginnings
SWALLOW – daring, freedom, grace
SWAN – transformation, intuition, grace, higher wisdom, inner beauty
TURKEY – blessings, generosity, service
VULTURE – death and rebirth, prophecy, great mother
WOODPECKER – industriousness, focus, sacred rhythms

amphibians and reptiles

CHAMELEON – adaptation, willingness to change, art of invisibility, sensitivity
COBRA – royalty, power, wisdom
CROCODILE/ALLIGATOR – ancient power, initiation
FROG – transformation, purification, new beginnings
LIZARD – guardian of the dream time, divination
SNAKE – wisdom, initiation, transformation, creativity, healing
TOAD – prosperity, abundance, earth spirit
TURTLE/TORTOISE – longevity, stability, home, Mother Earth

spiders and insects

ANT – industriousness, stamina, community

BEE – fertility, abundance, concentration, love

BEETLE/SCARAB – metamorphosis, creation, resurrection

BUTTERFLY – transformation, transmutation, joy, beauty

DRAGONFLY – dream messenger, joy, light

SPIDER – creativity, fate

mythical creatures

CENTAUR – mystical masculine power

DRAGON – immense spiritual power, protection

GRIFFIN – half-lion/half-eagle: provides connection between heaven and earth

PEGASUS – spiritual inspiration, grace, holiness

PHOENIX – transformation, rebirth, new beginnings

SATYR – half-man/half-goat: nature spirit, music, dancing, joy

SPHINX – half-human/half-lion: initiation, dark mother

UNICORN – love, gentleness, strength, purity

Colors

BLACK – introspection

BLUE – relaxation, meditation, peace

GREEN – healing, balancing

ORANGE – happiness, socializing

PINK – love, softness

PURPLE – royalty, intuition

RED – stimulating, activating, physical strength, passion

WHITE – purity

YELLOW – wisdom, communication, light of the sun

Index

For their contribution to this project, I would like to thank:

Claire Brown, my assistant and friend, for her love and for her devotion to this book.

Patricia Ridenour and her assistant, Iris Taboh, for the luscious photographs.

Susan Haifleigh, Sue Couri and Patricia Bloom for their encouragement.

Judith Kendra, editor extraordinaire, for her grace and kindness; Denise Bates and her assistant, Clare Johnson, for their generosity and care.

Catherine Bradley for her openness of heart that infused this book with spirit.

David Linn, my husband, and Meadow Linn, my daughter, for all of their love and support.

Claire Brown, Patricia Ridenour and Iris Taboh helped me prepare the altars for photography.

All the photographs in this book were taken by Patricia Ridenour, with the following exceptions: Images Colour Library 10-11, 16-17, 127, 147; Images/The Charles Walker Collection 46 left, 114, 115; The Bridgeman Art Library 15; The Garden Picture Library 78; Robert Harding Picture Library 30, 75; David Linn 60-61; Meadow Linn 7, 45, 130, 141.

The bagua maps on 94-95 were drawn by Susan Haifleigh.

About the Author

Denise Linn, a renowned lecturer, author and visionary, has researched healing traditions from cultures throughout the world for almost thirty years. With this wealth of knowledge, she originated the unique and groundbreaking therapeutic system Interior Alignment™. Her synthesis of practical information and spirituality has had a deep impact on thousands of participants worldwide. She is also the author of nine books, including *Sacred Legacies*, *The Secret Language of Signs*, *Quest*, and the international bestseller *Sacred Space*.

For information about Denise Linn's Interior Alignment™ practitioner course:

Denise Linn Seminars
P.O. Box 75657
Seattle, Washington
98125-0657

For Denise Linn tapes and videos:

QED
Lancaster Road
New Barnet
Herts EN4 8AS
England
www.qed-productions.com